HIS
WORDS

DARLA REED

FOR HIS CHILDREN

CONTENTS

FORWARD

It was opening day of Yankee Stadium, Friday the 13, 2012. The sky was picturesque, the energy was spectacular, the Yankees were about to take on the California Angels.

A giant American flag was unfurled by West Point cadets in the plush green grass of center field. The colors were marched onto the field by the West Point Color Guard with the overpowering white façade of Yankee Stadium, filling in as a big brother. As they started playing the "National Anthem", my eyes were misty as they always are, as I'm pleasantly reminded of my dear friend, US Army Officer and fellow coach, Joe Reed. Joe and I were basketball coaches at the US Military Academy where he shared with me his love for the flag and for West Point during our many drives around its spectacular campus. Thinking of Joe also reminded me that Doubleday Field at West Point is where Abner Doubleday founded baseball. Into the last stanza, "O'er the land of the free and the home of the brave," 2 Navy F-18 Super Hornets buzzed the stadium. Bedlam ensued as New Yorkers were jumping up and down, fired up for a new season of baseball. Meanwhile I was weeping like a baby, thanking my buddy Joe and all of his fellow soldiers who taught me the meaning of the word sacrifice. No greater gift can we receive than those men and women who have died so valiantly, so we can live in freedom.

Six days later through the power of social media, I got a message from Darla. She informed me of the book she has written about Joe.

Once again, I'm overcome with great gratitude. For my buddy, Joe was a special, special man, whose time with us was cut way too short. Joe loved many things, but his three most important loves were his faith, his family and his country.

I shared with Darla, the feeling I have every time I hear the "National Anthem". I am reminded of this friendly but stern lecture I received from Joe, about the importance of it and the symbolism that it evokes. It hit me again on Memorial Day, when I took my family to Baltimore to see not only the Orioles, but also Fort McHenry where Francis Scott Key wrote the Star Spangled Banner. The words in our National Anthem stir up even more emotion with the reminder of the battle which took place and of those who fought to defend their homes, their families and their freedom. A year before this battle, Major Armistead, commander of Fort McHenry, asked for a flag so big that "The British would have no trouble seeing it from a distance." Like John Hancock who signed his name on the Declaration of Independence big enough so the king would not need his spectacles to read it, Joe had that same confidence and bravado when he was fighting for something he believed in – the battle was now joined.

I'm so overjoyed that Darla has taken on this project. Joe was a once in a life time guy, who will now be remembered for all time.

I would ask you while reading this treasure, to grab a box of Kleenex and YouTube "The Battle Hymn of the Republic." Any version will do, my favorite so far is Judy Garland, but the last lyric blows me away when thinking of Joe Reed, the man, the father, the husband, the son, the officer, the coach, the friend.

"In the beauty of the lilies, Christ was born across the sea,

With a glory in his bosom that transfigures you and me.

As he died to make men holy, let us die to make men free,

While God is marching on."

Joe lived and died preserving our God-given right to freedom. There is no question, right now he is marching on and doing drills in heaven, watching over all of us and blushing that Darla would be so considerate to go out of her way for the children in preserving his legacy.

Tim O'Toole
ESPN College Basketball Analyst

ACKNOWLEDGMENTS

Thank you to Cathy Hill, who was the first person to tell me that I should write a book. Thanks to John Bytheway, who gave me the little push I needed with his talk on CD, "Turn off the TV and Get a Life!" He gave up late night TV in order to wake up early to write his first book. Thank you for continuing to inspire me and my children, John. I'm grateful to the Lord for waking me up at 4:30 the morning after I resolved to start. He continued to wake me up day after day, at that exact time. I was filled with energy and with a strong desire to write our story. I thank my mom and dad for raising me with love and trust and encouragement. I'm grateful to my siblings; (an amazing support group) Dawney, David, Dennis, Danette, Dale, Doug, and Diana and for their spouses; Gene, Kathy, Carolyn, Tim, Sharron, and Evan. A huge thank you to my editors: Mom, Danette, Kathy Baker, Enid Landry, and my professional editor, Ruth Pagan. You are true friends who sacrificed your precious time to edit and re-edit and edit again. An extra special thank you to Danette for the countless hours on the phone giving me feedback and encouragement and the prodding I needed. Thank you to Sharron Cathcart who gave me the idea to have everyone write to Joe's children after his death and for you and MegAnn's input on the book. Thank you to my niece, Wendy, who did the graphics on the cover and the blog. Thank you to my niece, Amber for your willingness to send me manuscripts during editing.

Thank you to Joe's parents, Mary and Joseph, for raising such an incredible individual. Your devotion and love for me and the children will never be forgotten. Thank you to Joe's sisters, Vonda and Daria, and their spouses, Damon and Corey for your love and time and support. Thank you to my cousin, Samantha for your friendship.

Thank you to my closest neighbors, Kayla and Alan Thurber, Kim and Bob Harrington, and Theresa and James Nally, who have all rendered service to me in my many moments in need.

Thank you to Agnes, my dear friend, who always understands me and helps me to understand others.

Thank you to my children, whose confidence in me has made me stand a little taller.

To Dawney, I don't claim to be a great writer, but any ability of writing I do have, can be traced back to that first journal you gave me so many years ago, thank you.

INTRODUCTION

"Many people idealize their loved ones after they die." The therapist kindly explained to me. He didn't understand. I talked about my husband that way when he was alive. Right after his death some of his friends and family members sent letters to our children, sharing something they remembered about Joe. This gave me proof that I wasn't just making it up. Their father really did live an exemplary life.

"I met Joe for the first time during church services at West Point. He was a cow (junior) and I was a new plebe (freshman). At West Point, the plebes must stand at attention and address the upper-class as Sir or Ma'am. Those rules changed, however, at church. At church we were all friends and called each other by our first names. I remember having a difficult time calling Cadet Reed by his first name because of his austere physical demeanor. Joe was tall and strong and he carried himself like he was a general (a rank that Joe would have easily attained). He simply commanded respect by his very presence. After being reassured several times that it was appropriate to call him Joe, we became very good friends."

Damon Owens

"I met Joe eight years ago at the United States Military Academy at West Point, New York. We played against one another in a basketball tournament. Joe was a cadet at West Point. Like most of the cadets, he was in excellent shape. He had been on the Army basketball team and he was a great player. He almost single-handedly whipped our team that day on the court. I was impressed by Joe. He was not only a gifted athlete, but there was much more to him. He played with real class and sportsmanship. He was having fun and his teammates were also enjoying the game – but not at our team's expense. They all played with sportsmanship. Joe was definitely the leader of their team. I immediately respected him. He smiled a lot. I'll always remember Joe's smile. The kind of smile that lights up and is contagious. He was confident yet sincere and genuine. I knew from that first encounter that Joe Reed was a good guy.

He was unselfish – passing the ball many times when he could have easily shot it in himself. He complimented players on both teams and offered his hand to help a player back to his feet after a fall. I've participated in and observed many competitive athletic events in my life and I'll never forget the first impression that I had of Joe. I thought – what a class act! We lost the game badly. I didn't care that much.

I wanted to meet this guy. After the game, he smiled and introduced himself. We sat on the floor in the gym. As we watched the next game, Joe told me about himself."

Kevin Doman

"Once when we went to Willcox for Doug's home coming, he took me for a walk, it was about a 45 minute walk and then he would talk to me and ask me how I was doing. He would always tell me how grades are important and should come first before sports. I always enjoyed talking to him and visiting with him."

Aaron Malaela

From the six page letter to the small note written by a 10 year old boy, all of these messages fit together like a puzzle, each letter a significant piece, revealing the whole portrait. Added to the letters from those who knew him are his own words in the form of hand written journal entries and multiple letters, as well as cassette tapes of him talking to me. These are a lost art but were the common choice of communication just one generation ago. I called these my letters from heaven. As I read and listened to his words from so long ago, I found advice and reassurance and pieces of his character that I had over-looked or had taken for granted. This book is a compilation of these words. This is the legacy he left for his children. This is our story.

CHAPTER 1
The End and the Beginning

At 7:00 AM the door bell rang. Not long before, J.R., my little three and a half year old boy, had climbed into bed with me. "What did you dream, Mommy?"

With my arm now around him, he burrowed into my side as I tried to share with him what I could remember of my dreams.

"I was in the commissary and then the cereal aisle turned into lockers at a school. I couldn't open my locker and I was late for class. And then I started to panic because I couldn't remember who was taking care of you and Jazi!"

J.R. giggled, "You're silly mommy!"

"Shh, we don't want Jazi to wake up yet," I reminded him. "What did you dream, J.?"

"Tigger took the honey pot from Pooh and I helped Pooh find it. I followed the bees and jumped like Tigger. And then I telled Tigger to give it back and he did. Then we had a party."

Just like his daddy, his dreams were one long adventure. Joe's dreams usually resembled a scene right out of one of his favorite Tom Clancy novels. I liked when he shared the movie that played in his head at night, especially when he acted it out. I remember one in particular, "I heard someone in the house, so I grabbed you and rolled us off the bed. I grabbed my gun as I low crawled across the floor to the bedroom doorway and stood up with my back to the wall. I peeked around the opened door to see him heading into the kids rooms. Before he knew what was comin' I put my rifle around his neck and put him to the ground. One punch was all it took to knock that knuckle-head out!"

I pulled my little "pooh bear" close and he held onto me tighter in response.

"Mommy, where'd daddy go?"

"Daddy went to Arizona to fly his helicopter." I whispered, knowing that once Jasmine sounded the alarm, my work day would have to begin. "Daddy will be able to see all our family in Arizona while he's there."

J.R. tried to climb on top of me but my growing belly didn't allow it, so he reluctantly returned to my side. I pictured my life in three short months: nursing my new born, eighteen month old Jasmine crying for her "baba" and my son wanting a hug, while "Mommy, Mommy, Mommy" played in surround sound. How would I juggle three children? I didn't have enough arms! Joe joked that we would have to switch from "man to man" to a "zone defense!"

So why was the doorbell ringing so early in the morning? A construction worker from across the street, I guessed. A new home was being built and I had had quite a few early morning visitors asking to use my hose to fill their water jugs. I slowly rolled out of bed, with J.R. by my side hugging my leg as I walked. I sighed with disappointment that our blissful introduction to the day had been interrupted.

I squinted through the peep-hole in the door. Three officers in dress greens, and Gina, the wife of our battalion commander looked back at me. Joe had left only four days ago. His battalion was going to Ft. Huachuca, Arizona for a month, to help with the border patrol. I was actually fine with him being gone for a month. I told him to write me love letters. I even looked forward to missing him and to anticipating our dramatic, romantic reunion. As the wife of the company commander, I took on the role of helping the wives in his company. I assured one wife who was very upset about a whole month without her husband, "It'll help him appreciate you and it'll be fun when he returns. It keeps your marriage exciting!" I had even organized a picnic for the wives that Saturday before, to help those who were already feeling lonely. Joe had tried to call while I was out. I was expecting him to call back that day or at least on Sunday, but he never did.

So here it was, Monday morning, and all of these military personnel were at my door. My stomach dropped, "Joe's been hurt," I thought as I opened the door.

One of the officers said, "Mrs. Reed, may we come in?"

Gina didn't say anything. We had become friends since we worked together, but as I looked to her for reassurance she quickly looked down.

"Has Joe been hurt?" I asked.

"Please sit down Mrs. Reed."

"Is he okay?"

"Please sit down Mrs. Reed."

I walked to the couch with all of them walking behind me. Gina sat by my side and the other officers sat on the love seat to my right. I was not prepared for what came next, "Joe must have had some serious injuries." I thought.

The same officer who had been the spokesperson knelt down on one knee and said, "Mrs. Reed, on behalf of the United States Army, we regret to inform you that your husband, Captain Joseph Oliver Reed III has been killed as a result of..."

What did he just say? I tuned him out. I just stared at him. He then started explaining that Joe's helicopter had collided with another. I was listening but I didn't feel what he was saying. I was saying to myself "No, that can't be right. This couldn't have happened to him. He's so strong. He's so safe. We studied the safety procedures almost every night."

"Ma'am, we're here to help you, we'll do whatever you need us to do."

I stared at him for awhile and said, "Could you leave?"

He replied quickly, "No ma'am, we won't do that. We'll be here for the day."

I really wanted everyone to leave. I just needed to be alone, to let this sink in, to be able to comprehend what he just told me. I felt like if they went away then this strange news would go away.

I searched the room as if searching for an answer. *How could this be? How could this happen? What*

will I do? Joe, where are you? How could this happen to you?
My wandering eyes stopped on the picture above the
fireplace. Joe had been driven to get that picture
framed and placed there. I was even thinking he was a
little too anxious about it. I had other priorities. Now,
that picture spoke to me like it never had before. It
was a picture of where we were married. It might look
like just a picture of a beautiful building to some, but
to a Mormon it's a symbol of our faith. In that
building, we were promised forever. Joe and I did not
say "till death do we part" when we were married in
that building, we said "for time and all eternity." It
was as if Joe were speaking to me now and reminding
me of this truth; that our union did not end with his
death. We would be together again as husband and
wife. A small amount of peace seeped into my
troubled heart as I gazed at the temple and then at the
small framed picture of our family, which I'd placed
in front of it on the mantle.

The officer interrupted my thoughts, "Ma'am,
where do you keep your important papers?"

"Everything is in the file cabinet, in our
bedroom. Is someone from the Army going to visit
my husbands' parents?"

"No ma'am."

"Then I have to call them." I got up and grabbed
the phone without even thinking it through, I just

started dialing, knowing I had to tell them. I hadn't even internalized what had happened when I was saying hello to Mamie.

"Mamie, is Pop there? Please get Pop on the phone."

Gina was sitting next to me. I don't remember if I waited for my father-in-law to get on the phone when I tried to say it, "Joe has been. . ."

I started to sob and handed the phone to Gina. I wish I would've had the strength to tell them, I wish I would've stayed on the line. But Gina was the one to break it to them. I quickly gained composure and took the phone, I remember hearing my father-in-law repeating, "Tell me it's not true, Darla, tell me it's not true!"

Suddenly everything and everyone seemed to be moving faster. I had to make a list of people I would want notified.

I went into our bedroom to call my parents. That's when I had to say the words. "Joe's helicopter went down and he was killed."

It felt like someone else was saying it. I broke down again, our conversation was short. They would call my siblings for me.

Once I had control of my emotions, I walked out

of the bedroom. I can't remember how many soldiers were in my home at the time, but they were entertaining the children. Jasmine had woken up and she was not at all disturbed by the crowd in our home. In fact, she was already jabbering with the soldiers and was thrilled that she had their undivided attention.

She has been social since day one. One time, while shopping in the commissary (she was just over one year old) I was letting her walk by the cart. While I decided on which can of green beans to get she disappeared. I frantically looked around, finally spotting her down at the other end of the aisle, jabbering away with a nice elderly couple. They were looking at her as if they understood every word. I frequently told people she spoke "Swahili." So as I walked into the front room Jasmine smiled at me and continued to bask in this rare moment of having such an attentive audience to entertain.

J.R. turned and ran to me to ask where I had been and why these men were in our house. As I looked at him I remembered his last moments with his daddy, "You take care of your mommy and your sister. You're the man of the house while Daddy is gone."

He stared at me, quiet and still in contrast to the commotion behind him. I took him back into our bedroom where I could concentrate on him. How could this little boy understand what I was about to say? How could I tell him his daddy wasn't coming home anymore? As I squatted down to be at his level, tears started flowing as I thought of what to say to my son.

"Why you crying Mommy?" He wiped my tears with his little fingers.

"J.R., Mommy has to tell you something."

"Are you sad?"

"Yes, Mommy's sad."

"Why are the soldiers here Mommy?"

"They came here to tell us what happened to Daddy." He just looked at me with those big beautiful brown eyes. "J.R., Daddy's helicopter fell out of the sky and he died, and he's in heaven now."

"Oh".

I could tell he couldn't grasp what I'd just told him. I couldn't even grasp what I'd just told him.

Our little talk was interrupted, "Ma'am, we have some questions for you."

The telephone rang continuously, forms to fill out, funeral service questions, where I want him to be buried, do I want him to be sent here to Ft. Bragg first? I just wanted everyone to go away, and I wanted to wake up from this nightmare.

My sister, Danette, was able to fly in that same day because she had been in Florida on a business trip. I love my sister, she's my dear friend. We hugged. She cried. I was numb, as if I were dreaming all of this, but in this dream I didn't have the luxury of jumping subjects like in my real dreams. She asked what she could do. I told her I needed to buy a black dress. A friend from church watched the children. Danette drove. As I walked into the PX I noticed people smiling and children laughing. A couple holding hands walked in front of us. I was so disturbed by everyone I saw; they were acting as if nothing had happened, as if the world was still moving when it had stopped for me. I had a strong urge to run out of the store. To keep from falling apart I focused on the goal of finding a nice black maternity dress and tried to block out all the annoying happy people. Danette kept me busy as she chose dresses for me to try on. I didn't let myself think about where I was going to wear this dress. I just focused on finding one I liked.

I can't remember how soon the rest of my family came but I remember my casualty assistance officer was helpful in picking everyone up. I have heard some terrible stories about widows who've had assistance officers who were very little help. I have to say, I was blessed with the best. Major Sneilson was a member of our church and knew of Joe, so he volunteered for the job. I think he went far and beyond his duty. He seemed to take care of everything, from picking people up at the airport to making sure I had all the benefits available to me. As he showed up that night after the last run to the airport, he asked me if he could give me a blessing. All worthy men in our church hold the priesthood and have authority to give blessings. He said he had been having promptings all day that the Lord had something he wanted me to know. I was definitely ready to hear what the Lord had to say so I quickly agreed. I don't remember all of the blessing but I do remember him saying that Joe had a great work to do and that it was in God's plan for him to be taken at this time.

I awoke way too early the next morning and when I remembered my new reality, I couldn't go back to sleep. I went back and forth from talking to God and then to Joe and sobbing at the thought of what had happened.

Joe, where are you? What are you doing right now? How could this have happened? I can't do this! How am I supposed to raise three children by myself? Why? Why? Why? Why did God take you? This wasn't supposed to happen! Why did You take him?

I wouldn't be able to address my Father in

Heaven without sobbing for a long time. Just getting on my knees would make all of my emotions come to the surface. I didn't hold back with Him. I couldn't hold it in. He knew what I was feeling anyway.

J.R. came in to cuddle and talk. How could I do this? Jasmine started crying. I didn't want to function, but I had to. I got up and I took care of my children. Before I could get them fed and dressed, my home was inundated with people: family and friends coming into town, flowers arriving, food being delivered, and calls coming in. Everyone seemed to be moving so fast. I was constantly interrupted the moment I began to think too hard about what had really happened.

"Ma'am, your husbands' belongings have arrived. Could you come make sure everything is here?"

Outside there was an Army vehicle of some kind, I sat on a little chair they provided by my front curb. A soldier gave me a list to check off the items as he transferred them from the vehicle into a box: his wallet, notebooks, uniforms, boots... I was anxious to have those things that were most recently in his possession. I thought maybe I would see a letter that he had started and then I saw that he had taken his journal. My heart jumped, maybe he wrote in it recently. I wanted some amazing entry, a message specifically to me. I anxiously opened it to see his last entry, but was disappointed to find the last date was just after Jasmine was born, a year previous. My heart settled back into its former position, somewhere close to my stomach, as I finished the task of checking the rest of the items off. Late that night I was able to thumb through and read Joe's journal. Though there was not a message written specifically to me, I discovered that every entry revealed an important part of him. Every entry he made was a precious message for me and for his children.

Joe's journal:

25 December 1994

It is Christmas day and as my family now rests from the excitement of the day I retire to read from the scriptures and ponder and pray. I am so blessed to have this beautiful family to love and care for. As I reflect on my younger days I am amazed that my life has taken such a course. A beautiful companion and two sweet children. A home that is warm and full of the temporal necessities... The Lord has blessed us immensely since we have been here in Alabama. I only pray that we will increase our obedience and faith to be worthy of his blessings in the future.

Every word I read made me sob, not only because of the thought of what has happened, but with gratitude for these precious words that I have, *his words*.

We had three funerals; the first was at our church, in Fayetteville. I was responsible for the whole program—music, speakers, printing the program—I wasn't ready for such a task. Even though I had my family and friends who helped me through it, I felt inadequate as I tried to think of a program that would be worthy of paying tribute to such a person. I knew Joe would like the opening song I chose, "Onward Christian Soldiers." One of Joe's best friends, Kevin, came from Utah to give the eulogy; Dave Bailey, a West Point friend, gave the sermon; and my brother and sister-in-law, Dennis and Carolyn, sang "Oh Lord, My Redeemer." I was grateful to Major Sneilson for asking a comrade of his to sing "How Great Thou Art." His voice was deep and beautiful.

The second service was on Post, Ft. Bragg, North Carolina, where we were stationed. As I was led in and took my seat, I faced a pair of boots with a gun standing in one of them and the helmet resting on the end of the gun. My heart still drops when I see this representation of a fallen soldier. His eulogy was given by our friend, Tim Thomas. Joe had served with him in the Army and in the Church while stationed at Ft. Riley, Kansas.

My family on both sides flew and drove to Florida to attend the third service at his family's church. It was a beautiful service. Another of Joe's best friends, Keith, gave the eulogy. At the end, a familiar tune was played, a song from the movie, "Glory." I associated this whole soundtrack with Joe. I had watched tears fall down his face while this music played at the end of the movie. We had attended a concert where the Harlem Boys Choir performed this song and we listened often to our cassette tape he had purchased. I wept as I heard the first four familiar notes.

J.R. was on my lap for all of the services. He kept his ears covered when people sang, and he wiped his face impatiently, "Mommy, you're getting me all wet!" he repeated numerous times—all those annoying tears. Jasmine stayed at home with friends and church members, she would have been climbing over the pews and chatting through it all.

His grave was dedicated by John Ribera, our dear friend and bishop from Ft Rucker, Alabama. The fly-by passed overhead, guns were fired, and the flag was handed to me.

I was there but it didn't feel like it was my

experience. It felt more like a movie I had a front row seat to, like the one Joe and I watched one Saturday afternoon on TV, "The Great Santini." The man of the house was a Marine fighter pilot. He dies in the end. Why did Joe make me watch those darn movies? I didn't like watching sad-ending movies. I liked happily–ever-after movies. That's what our story was going to be—a happily-ever-after story. I thought the trials we had had up till then were going to be the worst we would have or at least if it got worse, we would handle it together. How could I handle the challenges of this life alone?

Every night my mind played the movie I wanted to be in. Joe was back, he had been on a secret mission, "Sorry I couldn't tell you about it sweetheart." It was always some crazy explanation for the Army faking his death. The worst part was waking up. The questions I had been asked would play in my head, *Where are you going to live, where are you going to have the baby, are you going to sell the house, are you going to stay here?* Praying was my only option. I had to make these decisions, and I had to go where God wanted me to go. After all, He's the one who put me in this position, and He would now be the only one who could lead me through it. I pled for guidance every moment I had alone.

Flashbacks now took up a majority of my thoughts. We were sitting at our kitchen table. Joe told me that he thought, "This could be it," every time he flew, "I make sure things are right between God and me and my family before every take off." This had disturbed me. I never worried about him dying, and it surprised me that he considered it every time he flew.

Before we moved to Ft. Bragg, Joe had arranged for us to see many friends and family. I now thought back in amazement, he saw every important person in his life in such a short time. We traveled from Ft. Rucker, Alabama to Arizona to Utah and weeks later, to our destination, North Carolina.

J.R. had just turned three and Jasmine was nine months old. I will never forget the pleadings from them to get out of their car seats—this was the era before VCR and DVD players in cars, and oh how we suffered! When we were about to arrive at our first destination in Texas, I looked back to see blank, zombie-like stares from two little people who had lost their fight. It was really sad but it made us laugh! We made many stops along the way, introducing important people to each other; people who had touched our lives.

We stayed the night in Texas with a special family I was thrilled to introduce to Joe. Brother and Sister Hassell, my mission president and his wife, were like parents to me while I was on a mission. I learned so much from them and looked up to them.

It made me so happy for them to meet Joe. From there we drove to Arizona to see all of my family. We then headed north and stopped in northern Arizona and southern Utah to see Bishop Ribera's daughters and parents. Also in Utah I was able meet the Hammonds, they were missionaries who taught Joe in Florida. We stayed with the Doman's, our dear friends, and Joe got to meet my Uncle Marvin and Aunt Uni, as well as cousins, Dan and Perry. I was grateful they got to meet Joe and know what an amazing person he was. And on our way from Utah to North Carolina we stopped in Kentucky to visit Chris and Kevin Hub, some friends from our time in Kansas.

We also went to a family reunion in New Jersey before moving into our house and we spent Christmas with his family in Florida that year. It was all his doing, all his idea to travel so extensively that year. I'm sure he was inspired, not knowing the reason why.

Joe had made changes over the years but as I think back now of significant moments I had with him, it seemed the months before he died, were extraordinary. Joe was so calm when I announced I was pregnant, even though we had not planned it. I was worried and overwhelmed and was anticipating him being even more stressed than I. He surprised me when he said it would be okay, we could handle it.

His only worry was "putting them all through college at the same time."

Just a month before, when I had gotten into a small car accident, which was my fault, I stressed the whole way home as I anticipated having to tell Joe. His reaction was a relief. Instead of getting upset with me, he said, "Don't worry about it. I'm just grateful you and the kids are all right." An unexpected hug replaced an expected lecture. A gradual change had taken place in my husband. He was calm, even though he had so much more to do now. He had just taken command of a company, and he had just received a leadership calling in our church; a counselor to the bishop. He had goals to earn his masters degree, he had two children who wanted his attention as soon as he walked through that door every night, and he had a wife who also wanted so much more attention than he could ever give her.

My favorite flashback, well it actually was the flashback that made me cry the most, but it seemed to be the one my mind liked to play over and over again, was when I last saw him. He was in his flight suit, he kissed us all goodbye and as he walked away toward the hanger, I stayed and watched. He turned around and waved once and then he kept walking. I was glad it was a little bit of a walk to the hanger because I enjoyed watching my husband with his back to us. He always walked like a soldier. His feet came well up off the ground with each step, his broad shoulders were squared, and his head up. His flight suit showed off his V-shape, he was my invincible G.I. Joe. I had grown to love and admire him more and more. He said his goodbyes and now he was walking away from us, a symbolic image which played in my mind now.

I wished we would have been able to talk that weekend. I already had so much I wanted to share with him. The same day we said goodbye, I took J.R. and Jasmine on Post for free horse rides. J.R. hadn't gone a day without wearing his boots since Joe's Mom had bought them for him and he talked about being a cowboy all the time. At the corral he stood on the bottom section of the wooden fence, holding onto the top section as he watched others get their turn to ride. His smile took up his whole face he was so excited to be there. Equipped with his boots and hat, he walked toward the horse but as he got closer the horse grew bigger, his eyes widened as he looked all the way up.

"I no can do it, Mommy, I scared!" he yelled as he started backing up. I tried to talk him into it, I even tried to lift him up so the horse wasn't so intimidating but he wasn't having it.

As we walked away he hung his head and slowly said, "I thought I was a cowboy."

I hugged him and told him he was still a

cowboy, he just needed a horse more his size. I wanted to share that with Joe. He would've had the same feelings of sympathy for the little guy but it would've cracked him up too. Who will I share things like that with now? No one else will care as much or understand as well. How could I live without sharing everything with my husband?

I thought I had had some intense cries before my husband died; they were nothing like the way I cried now, like my insides would come out.

CHAPTER 2

From the Beginning

As a young girl, I always wondered who I would marry. I wondered what he would be like, and how many children we would have. I never, in all my dreams, imagined being a widow. I never imagined that the man I would marry would be so dang tall, dark and handsome either. I was born in a small town in Arizona, a very small town. How did my husband and I meet? I couldn't have ever imagined such a love story!

I was the fifth of eight children: Dawney, David, Dennis, Danette, Darla, Dale, Doug, and Diana, or as my father liked to call her, "De-end." My father was a social studies, civics, and P.E. teacher. He was not only a teacher; he was also a coach for more than one sport, the city pool manager in the summer, a State Farm insurance agent, and a tax agent as well. He also helped with major repairs on the school during the summer. Dad could do anything and knew everything. He was our encyclopedia, math tutor, and "spell check." I loved to go watch my father play softball because he hit a homerun almost every game. He did trick shots when playing basketball, bouncing it into the hoop or shooting backwards. One time, as my high school basketball coach, he said we could stop doing suicides and jumping drills if he made the next shot. He was at half court, we had a little hope that he'd make it, then he shot behind his head and we lost all hope. Dad was even amazed as we all heard the *swish!* We jumped for joy!! He smiled at the other coach and shrugged his shoulders.

My mother worked for the Willcox School System also, in the front office of the high school and in the library. She also managed to feed and clothe eight children! She sewed most of our clothes. My favorite jeans were ones she sewed with yellow leather stars on the back pockets with leather that had been given to her. Mom was a pro at finding deals, buying in bulk and preserving food for our crew. Sometimes a farmer in the area would let us pick corn, as much as we wanted. I remember husking, chopping, bagging, and freezing till I didn't want to see corn ever again. I was also familiar with cherry pitters, a small metal gadget that pushes the pit out of the cherry. We had two peach trees, an apricot tree and a garden. At a certain time of the year we would have zucchini everything from enchiladas to chocolate cake. My mom wouldn't let us know zucchini was one of the ingredients until after we had eaten it. When the peaches were in season we would have waffles with peaches and whip cream made with eggs and cream we bought fresh from a family who lived "out in the country." This used to seem so far away but it was actually only around 5 miles out of the city limits. We ate organic, cage free and non-homogenized before I knew what all that meant! I didn't know how good I had it!

Everyone knew us; we all had the same skinny build, and the same blonde hair and blue-eyed look. I never had trouble with anyone because I think they were afraid of my 6'3", 235-pounds-of-muscle father. One guy told me that I wasn't being asked out because of my dad's calves. He said they were like the Hulk's calves and all the guys were afraid my dad would "Hulk out" on them. We had a family that was a little like "Leave it to Beaver", except it was a little more chaotic with all eight of us. I always thought my life was so hard because we weren't rich. I wanted to have new store-bought clothes and Ding-Dongs and Twinkies in the cupboard like my friend had. But as I look back, I can see how rich we were—rich with security and love and trust and respect. My parents gave to us spiritually and emotionally more than money could buy.

I didn't travel too far when I went to college, just an hour's drive away to the junior college my father had attended, as well as all my siblings ahead of me. Many professors and administrators knew that I was a Cathcart, so I continued to be a bit sheltered even as I went off to continue my education. I was also eased into college life by living with my older brother and sister, Dennis and Danette. We all shared a studio apartment with bunk beds for Danette and me, and a single bed for Dennis. We had one open closet and one bathroom. It took a little getting used to.

One time as I scanned our closet for what to wear, Dennis said, "Don't turn around!"

Of course I turned around as I said, "Why?" and then I quickly jerked my head back and tried to erase the picture I had of my brother in nothing but a jock strap, trying to cover himself as much as he could with his hands and arms.

"What are you doing?"

"I am getting undressed in my bedroom!"

"It's my bedroom too!!"

"I forgot!"

My brother and sister made everything about going to college a little easier: registering, getting involved with the LDS Institute, meeting friends, as well as getting a job with the basketball coach. Being involved with sports was a part of my life. I loved volleyball, basketball, softball, and tennis. Back in high school, I was lucky to have been raised in a small town where I had a better chance of making the school teams. My dad's notoriety probably helped too. Even though I was pathetically skinny and awkward they knew I had potential. Because I became a pro at cheering my team on from the sidelines, I tried out for the cheerleading squad. All those years of bench warming paid off! All my electives involved exercise: swimming, weight training, volleyball, aerobics, and cheerleading. My academic advisor once said, as he looked at my schedule, "It seems you are in good physical condition… but are you going to graduate?!"

Well, I did graduate with an associate's degree and with memories of the best social life I'd ever had. My father used to say in a teasing way, "I hope you're not letting your studies interfere with your social life." I didn't! I dated a lot and had tons of good clean fun. The after-the-game dance was the highlight of my week. That's when I discovered I really could dance. I was just brought up with the wrong type of music! I also discovered the black guys made the best dance partners. I really enjoyed learning all the dances of the day. My favorite was "the smurf." For being raised in a town full of cowboys, it was amazing how much "soul" I had up in me!

When my junior college fun days were coming to a close, I had to decide what I was going to do next. I had made some significant changes my second year of college. I became a little more serious about my spiritual growth. I started to pray every morning and every night on my knees. I really talked to God and asked him for help and guidance. I also read scriptures every morning before my 6:00 AM aerobics class (this was after I had socialized and then started my homework at midnight, I think I was bionic at the time.) I mention this change I had made because I think it was significant. As I look back on my life, I know that God was guiding me, and I don't think He could have if I hadn't been praying sincerely and reading His words.

My sister and I used to call these daily rituals: "the Sunday School answers." If the teacher called on us and we had no idea what was just asked or even what the subject was, we could say; "pray always" or "read your scriptures," and we were always right. We would laugh about it, experimenting in the class room with our theory. We thought we were pretty hysterical.

For example, the teacher would ask, "What would you do if some friends wanted you to drink with them…Darla?"

Since I was in la la land and was not listening until my name was called, I would say, "Pray?"

Then the teacher would say, "Um….yes, praying first would be a great thing to do." We could get the answers right without listening. We thought we had the teachers fooled, but it turns out that we were the fools. I hadn't experienced much in my life at that point, but oh how I have discovered that those "Sunday School answers" *are* the best answers to all of life's questions!

The last few months of school, my mind was taken over by the question of where I would go next, and what I wanted to be when I grew up. (I am still stewing over that question!) I was a lifeguard at the college pool that year, and while at work I approached some girls I hadn't seen before. They told me they had just gotten back to town from New York where they had been nannies. I was so intrigued by what they had experienced that I wanted to hear all about it. I was so jealous of them and wished I could travel far away from this small area and see the other side of the country! As I expressed my interest, one of them said she could put me in touch with her previous employer and see if she would hire me. Within days, I had a job offer. It seemed to work out so effortlessly, and there wasn't any part of me that thought it wasn't a good idea to take the job. That's how I think the

Lord answered my prayer. He made it so I felt extremely confident that what I was doing was the right thing to do.

I didn't appreciate my parents enough when I was leaving for New York, but I can understand a little more now, how hard it must have been for them to let me go. They were so worried. I later contemplated their amazing parenting. They taught me how to be responsible and to make decisions for my own life and then they LET me! What if they would have been controlling and forced me to go to a specific university that they had chosen for me, it might have changed my whole life. I'm grateful to them for letting me learn I had it in me to make good choices for my own life.

The Coopers picked me up at the airport. I was almost 20 years old and it was my first time to fly, not counting the couple times my Uncle Bob took our family for a ride in his small plane. What a different world I was stepping into—culture shock comes to mind. Terry, the mother, introduced her children: Joshua and Abigail, and we headed to the city to meet the father of the family, Douglas Cooper. Oh my goodness I was going to New York City! Everything was amazing and new and fascinating to me! The tall buildings, the homeless leaning up against them, so many people, "Two for fi' dolla'!" was yelled out above the noise of the cars honking at each other. We passed a guy being handcuffed, a small crowd had formed, and a man in a strong New York accent yelled out, "Keep movin', keep movin', happens every day!" Not in my world it didn't! After meeting the man of the house, we all went to Little Italy to have dinner. It was a feast for my eyes as well as my stomach, too many things to look at. I knew I would need to come back in order to take it all in.

The Coopers made me feel comfortable, I felt like I was the big sister. Abby liked to play Barbies and play in the kitchen, combining her choice of ingredient's to make a "cake." Josh liked to play catch, and as I drove them around town he knew right away when I was lost! Doug was hysterical. He was always making me laugh. When he teased his wife, she would say, "Oh Douglas, stop it!" Terry was so kind. It was easy to like her. They were Jewish by birth but shared with me one night at dinner that they didn't believe in God. Doug told me that they believed we would die like the trees die and we would rot in the ground like one too. Terry didn't like his explanation, "Oh Doug, she doesn't want to hear that!" I don't think I'd ever met anyone who didn't believe in God before. My belief in God was so much a part of my world. I couldn't fathom life without this belief. One time I asked Terry what motivated her to be so nice if she didn't believe in God or in an after-life. She said she believed that what we give, we get back in return – karma.

Before coming to live with them, I had visions of driving a Benz or a Volvo. I just knew this wealthy family would have nothing but high-end cars to drive. Well, that dream was crushed when they showed me the copper colored Gremlin I would be driving. I later learned to appreciate that Doug and Terry were brought up in wealthy homes and were a bit disgusted with those who flaunted their affluence. They didn't need to drive a new Jaguar to feel good about themselves. In fact they seemed to enjoy flaunting their economical cars.

We lived right around the corner from a synagogue. I worked there over the summer as the "Creative Movement Specialist" for summer camp. I led groups of children in Big Bird aerobics. I learned to like boiled eggs and cheese pizza. Doug and Terry taught their children all of the Jewish traditions and holidays. They went to synagogue on special occasions. On the Sabbath, cars would line up on our street and people would walk around the corner to the synagogue. One day when friends of theirs parked in front of their house and commenced to walk around the corner, Doug pointed out a family of Orthodox Jews who followed the law of not driving on the Sabbath. They had walked all the way from their home. He then yelled out to his friends, "Why did you park here and walk instead of just parking at the synagogue?"

"Oh Douglas, stop!" Terry came up behind him as he continued to ask the question loud enough for all to hear. Doug continued to make me laugh.

Terry started to encourage me to go to West Point soon after I arrived. Other girls who worked for her had gone and had loved it so much that they kept going back regularly. I didn't know anything about West Point or why I would want to go…so I didn't, until 6 months later. Early December some friends who frequented the Point talked enough about a great dance they had there every weekend that I decided to go with them. I was amazed with the beautiful campus, but because it was finals time, the dance wasn't all that great and I wasn't planning on returning.

Being home for Christmas meant so much more that year. I had really missed my family. I wasn't quite ready to head back to New York but I had made a commitment for one year and I would honor that commitment.

In February our church group was invited to go to West Point for a tour. Why would the Mormon cadets at West Point choose to invite a ward (congregation) which was an hour's drive away? I will tell you—because there were about 100 girls, ages eighteen to twenty-three in that ward, I wasn't the only one coming from the West to be a nanny! We even had our own bishop and relief society (women's group) because we were just too much for one leader to handle.

I wasn't going to go because I hadn't enjoyed myself before, but some friends pushed the issue enough that I gave in. February 21, 1987, I drove up to West Point, totally unaware of how this day would affect the rest of my life. Touring the campus this time helped me to appreciate the history of West Point. Having a cadet explain the significance of the statues, the parades, and the great men each building was named after made the place even more impressive. I was disappointed though, that the tour didn't include the gym. I begged the cadets to show us where the gym was, so they escorted us to a huge building with more than one gym, more than one weight room, more than one everything you would need to work out!

I was in my element now. I looked around like a child would look around Disney World. I was not only impressed by all the equipment, the athletes weren't bad to look at either! A volleyball tournament was taking place. I was in heaven! I watched a couple games and then wandered into a gym where some guys were shooting around. One guy, a nice looking black guy, was dunking it.

I let out a loud "Woohoo" without thinking— my cheerleading days you know. He turned to look at me so I said, "How about doing one backwards?" He obliged, and he added a wink as it went through! I let out another cheer. I probably jumped up and down too, like a bebop cheerleader would. I didn't stay there long though. I wanted to play a little "pepper" with a friend (that's a little one-on-one volleyball game.)

That night the Mormon cadets had planned a dance, separate from the dance hall I had gone to before. I wasn't having the best time there and my friend, Lisa had already attached herself to a cadet. So when Lisa asked if I wanted to go to "Ike," which was the main dance, I accepted.

It was packed! One of my favorite songs, "Lean on Me," by Club Nouveau, started playing. I had to dance. I had to do "the wop," which was just the right dance for that song. I was on my own so I started for the dance floor, looking almost frantically for someone to dance with. "Gotta dance, gotta dance, gotta dance..."

As I pushed through the crowd I heard someone say, "I was dunking it for her today." I turned and saw the nice looking black guy I had seen earlier that day. I thought "Perfect! My dance partner."

"Would you like to dance?" Again, he obliged. After dancing a few fast ones, a slow song came on. He smiled at me and held out his hand, I took it and we started to sway together effortlessly. He swayed just the right way, with a little extra step on each side. I remember thinking "Now this is the way to slow dance." I was hoping he wouldn't mind if I wanted to dance with him for the rest of the evening. After a couple slow songs played, a fast song came on and we hesitated a bit as we held each other.

I felt so comfortable with him. We elected to leave the dance floor to get a drink. Conversation came easy. He had a great smile, a great attitude about life. He talked about his family and his upbringing. I really enjoyed his company. We went out on a balcony to be able to hear each other better. I was comfortable with him holding my hand as we walked. I was also comfortable as we exchanged phone numbers and he gave me a good night kiss! There was something special about this guy. His name seemed so average to me, Joe Reed. But I soon found out that there was nothing average about this Joe!

CHAPTER 3

The Past....my favorite place to go

After Joe died, it was really hard to look to the future. I didn't let myself think about my life without him. The past became my favorite place to be. I would take frequent trips there whenever time permitted. Sadly though, daydreaming was a luxury. I felt like I was being pushed to move at an uncomfortable pace.

We were living in Spring Lake, North Carolina. We had just bought our first house just seven months prior and were still settling in and getting used to the Fayetteville / Ft. Bragg area. We were just starting to meet our neighbors. After Joe's death, I was able to know what caring and unselfish neighbors we had. One man, who had previously suffered the loss of his own son, came over to speak kind words to my mother-in-law. At the same time, his wife and a few others went around the neighborhood to collect money for me. I was so touched by this gesture. People I didn't even know had given twenties and written checks and had given so freely. There was almost $400 there. The money was appreciated, but even more meaningful was the idea of each twenty dollar bill representing someone who cared. They were neighbors in the true sense. I will never forget their kindness.

Kayla, a neighbor I met at church, had become my close friend in the short time we lived there. We called each other daily, babysat for each other, borrowed from each other's pantries, and enjoyed each other's company. Her husband, Alan, had become friends with Joe, and we enjoyed many meals together, including Thanksgiving dinner.

While I was in Florida for Joe's funeral, Kayla hung up all the flowers I had been given and gave me the idea of putting them into a dry flower arrangement. I appreciated all the flowers that were sent to me and grateful to be able to preserve the kindness of friends and family.

I also appreciated those who did things that were a little out of the ordinary. Instead of flowers, one person gave us a gift bag full of activities for the children: toys, coloring books, crayons, and an enormous pop-up book, which is still at my in-laws home for the grandchildren. It's a great reminder of their thoughtfulness. Another person ran all my errands, i.e.... dry cleaners, developing photos, and groceries. My sister-in-law, Sharron, gave me the idea to ask Joe's friends and co-workers to write a letter to our children describing their father's character. I started receiving letters right away from a variety of people who all helped to paint a portrait of a man his children would someday want to know.

I would have to leave this area, these friends, this new home. Staying was not an option. With both of my previous pregnancies I had had complications, and had been put on bed rest. We were already taking precautions in anticipation of similar complications, so I knew I would not be able to be alone. I decided to go live with my parents until my baby was born. That would give me time. Trying to decide where I was going to live at that point was far too overwhelming. I didn't even want to think about setting up a home without Joe. My dear father stayed and helped me sell the house. My church family, under Kayla's direction, cleaned the house and planted flowers in front. The task of separating what I would send to Arizona and what I would put into storage was beyond my ability. Kayla rescued me. She took charge and pushed me through the task. I thank God for friends and family who carried me through these paralyzing moments.

Within a month I was back in my childhood home, wondering what the heck I was doing there. I was grateful to have loving supportive parents, but I didn't want to be there, and of course they didn't want that for me either. Although J.R. became Grandpa's little right hand man, he kept asking where his daddy was. I tried to keep him busy with swimming lessons and he even got to have the chance to "be a cowboy." He wasn't so intimidated with a small pony. But the activities weren't enough of a distraction. He still wanted to go back to his "lellow house in Car-o-lina" and play with his daddy.

At any given time, usually when he was frustrated about something or when he was tired, he would cry uncontrollably and yell, "I don't want it, I don't want it, I don't want it...." Sometimes I would hold him and join in, I didn't want it either!

I thought I better talk to someone to help me know what to do for him. I was fortunate to find a great therapist right there in Willcox. Victoria helped me understand that this was the only way J.R. could grieve because he didn't cry himself to sleep as I did. She advised me to let him get it out but to not let him go on for too long. This helped me and my parents to be a little more patient when he had his outbursts.

Jasmine became my little comic relief. She was starting to form understandable English words in between her native Swahili language. She was showing signs of wanting to be a table dancer which worried me a bit. I hoped this wasn't a look into her future career choice. She was constantly trying to get on the table to dance. When we would let her, she would perform a dance she had made her own. We called it, "The Jazz." She would tuck one arm against her chest, cock her head and turn slowly as she bounced to the music and the rhythm of us chanting, "Go Jazi, go Jazi, go go go Jazi!" She had performed this same dance for her daddy—on the floor. She didn't seem to know anything was wrong, she laughed and played and brought a little happiness to my saddened spirit.

Mom and Dad did everything they could to make me comfortable and keep me from doing too much. It was like living at the perfect hotel with a restaurant where I could order whatever my heart desired. If I decided I would really love a turkey dinner, mom would have started preparing. Dad was ready to take me anywhere I needed to go. My siblings were also very supportive and ready to help. But they just couldn't make it all better. They couldn't bring Joe back. This was what I desired most and it was work to care about anything else.

At night, when everyone else was asleep, I would pray, read Joe's journal and sob until I fell asleep. I usually woke up at 3 or 4 in the morning to repeat the ritual. I felt close to him when I read his words and touched the pages he had touched, and I imagined him reading to me. I could go back in time; I could be with him again.

Joe's version:

It is 23 May 1987 and this is my first entry into a journal I hope to keep for the rest of my life. I am now 21 years old, born 21 Feb 1966. I have been inspired to keep this journal because of the appearance of a special young lady that has entered into my otherwise boring life. Darla. So that I may catch up with myself let me state that I am a cadet at West Point just finishing up my second year.

On 21 Feb. 1987 I turned 21 years old. It was a Saturday and I was quite disappointed because I had just turned 21 on a Saturday and I had to spend it at good old West Point. Well that day I decided to be by myself and sulk.

That afternoon I decided to go and lift weights, when I was finished I walked into the Central Gym where some good ball was being played. I only had on my reebok aerobic sneakers and

I knew that if I played I may turn my ankle. But after watching awhile I went to a side basket and began shooting around. Naturally I got a little warmed up and started dunking; tossing a few down when the lane was open. Just as I threw one down pretty solid I heard a voice say, "Yeah Dunk it." I looked over to the sideline and a few girls had just walked in escorted by a few cadets. The one who spoke was tall and had blonde hair; she was showing her friends how I was slamming. Of course I had to show off. After a few more jams she went about her business and I got picked up for a few games. A guy named Jeff Bergman, later, pointed this same girl out and said, "Joe that is what I want for my birthday." I said in return, "Well heck, today is my birthday, how 'bout getting that for me." Little did I know how true my wish would come.

That night I decided to go down to Ike and celebrate my birthday by myself by treating myself to a sub and milkshake. So I got dressed up in my Blazer and headed for Ike. For some reason or another I felt different that night, as if I were in some kind of

Nirvana. Well I got to Ike and ate my dinner.

Sarks was down there so I started rapping with him and Mark Hannon. We were, as usual, evaluating the Ike chicks. It was a good night for girls, better than usual. About that time some nice looking girls walked in and Sarks took notice exclaiming "Who is that!!!" Remembering them from the gym I said, "I saw them in the gym while playing ball." The tall blonde heard me and said Hi. She then looked at the dance floor and then looked at me and asked me to dance. I was shocked. I was so stunned that all I could say was "yeah, I guess so."

She could really dance; she was doing the WOP and what not. I asked her, her name and she said Darla. (I forgot her name shortly after.) After we danced we went and talked for awhile. She was working as a Nanny in New Rochelle, she's from Willcox, Arizona. We spent the rest of the evening together talking and dancing. When it got late we exchanged phone numbers and addresses. I then got up the nerve to kiss *her good-night. I don't know how I get these surges of boldness, but it sure is great.*

Joe called me a few days after we first met and promised another call a few days later. I decided if I was going to start dating this guy, I better let him know about my religion. I had had bad experiences in the past with dating guys who didn't appreciate the values I held and I didn't want to play that game again. So, I wrote him a letter letting him know I was Mormon and that my religion was very important to me. I told him I didn't drink, wouldn't have sex before marriage, and when I married, I wanted it to be forever, in a Mormon temple. I also mentioned I had plans to serve a mission for my church. I wondered if I would get a call back, but I thought if he didn't call, then it just wasn't meant to be.

He called. He also wrote me back:

Dear Darla   *6 March 1987*

I know by now we probably would have talked on the phone, but I felt compelled to write you back from your first letter. By now I have read it about 10 times and every time it seems to get better.

I don't know what it is that is compelling me to tell you the things I do either, I guess you must be special too. Don't worry about not telling me you were Mormon, because it would not have made a difference. How could I be biased or partial to what your religion was, when obviously it makes no difference to you that I am Black. (You did notice I hope)☺!! You see I could tell right away whether you would've been bothered by it or not by the way you would have acted when we were walking around holding hands.

Oh yeah, I am glad you mentioned the subject of what I expected of our relationship, because I want to address that issue. I will never make more of it than what you want it to be. All I want is to be with you as much as possible, so we can enjoy each others company. I don't know how far my feelings for you will go, I suppose it is going to be difficult when June rolls around. But it is something I chose to accept when you said you had to go back the first time we met. You are just too incredible 'a girl to pass up, ya know! And don't worry, I'd have to be insane to bag *somebody that the mere thought of brightens up my day! (Picture of a sun) It has gotten to a point now that my roommate knows when I am thinking of you.*

Joe was intrigued with my values and goals and wanted to know more about what Mormons believe. I must say that I was a little overwhelmed with telling him about what I believe. All my life I had learned so many things, it was hard to know where to begin.

"What do Mormons believe?"

"Well, let's see, no drinking, no smoking, Jesus Christ and Heavenly Father, prophets, temples, the Book of Mormon and the Bible..."

It was easier if he had questions that I could answer because I really didn't know where to start. One discussion we had was about him when he was a baby. He said when he was born, there were complications and they were worried he wouldn't live. He was read his last rights just in case. He said, "I always wondered if I had died, would I have gone to hell because I hadn't been baptized?"

I responded with, "Do you really think God would send a perfect, innocent baby to hell and another to heaven just because one had not been baptized and the other had?" I shared my belief that all babies are innocent and pure and do not need to be baptized and that when babies die, they go straight back to God because they are perfect and don't need to stay here to be tested. This idea intrigued him and he wanted to understand more of what my church believed.

For the next few months we got together maybe a total of six times, most of our getting to know each other was over the phone and in letters. He wasn't like any guy I had ever met. He was so thoughtful and concerned with my happiness and welfare. He would tell me exactly when he was going to call and he was never a minute off. I was also impressed with his beautiful penmanship!

We continued to talk about my faith. Every time we spoke, I would find out he had attended a church meeting or he had spent the day with the Mormon missionaries, or he had found yet another friend or professor who was Mormon. His Spanish professor was not only Mormon but had lived in Willcox as a young boy! Joe thought that was a crazy coincidence! It's good he didn't rely on me alone to find out about the church.

A couple months after we met, he asked me about a picture he saw in a Mormon friends' room. He was interested to know the story behind this "warrior-looking dude with massive, muscular arms, who was kneeling with such a humble look on his face." I was happy to tell him about Moroni, the last prophet who wrote in the Book of Mormon. Moroni was preparing to bury the records which had been kept by previous prophets over a span of about a thousand years. He was definitely a warrior; his whole life was about war. The next time Joe and I saw each other, I gave him a copy of the book.

Dear Darla,   *3 May 1987*

Thanx for a great weekend! It seems every time I see your smiling face ☺ it gets better and better...

When I got back to my room I read what you put on the inside of the Book [of Mormon], and I was very pleased! I will read it along with the Bible, something I definitely need to get back too.

My curiosity of you is great now that I am dying to learn about what makes you tick!! [In a Mormon friend's room] I saw a picture of the Holy Bible and The Book of Mormon. I guess I found what I was looking for because I want to see where everything fits into some kind of scheme. That is something we can talk about on either Tues. or Wed. night, so do your research and be ready to fill me in. Alright!

I think we need to talk more about our after - graduation; mission - relationship. I know how you feel and what you want and don't want, but at this point I think we would be making a terrible mistake not to at least try for something!! I don't know maybe I am just caught up in the moment. But I do know that come May 27 that it will not be the last time you see or hear from me.

Joe started reading The Book of Mormon right away. He also talked with the missionaries there so they could answer all his questions. The next time I was at West Point, we were on a path walking up a hill, with a thin iron handrail lining the path. Joe commented that this was just like Lehi's dream with the path and the iron rod (this is a dream a prophet relates where everything is symbolic of our journey through this life.) His understanding of what he was reading surprised me. This was the first time I'd given the book to someone and had actually gotten feedback, as well as a seminary-type discussion about the deep meaning of the stories and doctrine taught.

The times we were together were few and far between, but they were all memorable. We had picnics and we took long walks around West Point ("Flirtation Walk," was the name of the path we would take) but my favorite dates with him involved dancing. "Ike" was nice but that was nothing in comparison to the times when he would bring his boom box to a park or on a pier and we would dance under the stars. Luther Vandross and Freddie Jackson played a huge role in our evenings together, though our favorite song at the time was "Always" by Atlantic Star. Joe made a tape for both of us with our favorite songs so that when we weren't together, we could listen to it and daydream about dancing together.

I can't remember how soon I called home and mentioned to my mother that I had this "friend" who I was spending time with. I was afraid to tell her we were dating. It was understood in our home that we should not date people of another race, "You marry who you date and marriage is hard enough and you don't need to complicate things." They never said anything negative about people of other races. They just accepted that marrying another race would bring too many differences, which invited problems into a marriage. I was questioning this concept now. Joe and I didn't seem to be that different at all.

After speaking with my mother and getting a

negative reaction from her, I felt troubled. I liked pleasing my parents. I was also still wondering how far this was going to go and I wasn't sure how I felt about Joe and me being together in the future. I went up to my room and got on my knees. I asked my Father in Heaven if he cared if Joe and I were different races, if it even mattered, and if He approved of us spending time together. After waiting in silence for a short time, the feeling within me changed from being troubled to being at peace. I knew what I felt at that moment was from God. How else could my worry be replaced with a good feeling so instantly? I knew I had God's approval to continuing to see Joe.

One weekend Joe took me to meet his extended family. He had grandparents, aunts and uncles who lived on the Jersey Shore. I was happy to be introduced to this world so different from the one I grew up in. I smiled as we drove through this small Jersey town with two and three story homes. I loved the quaint look of the houses; all different colors, close together with porches and streets filled with people, most of them black. The last time I had been in an all black area was when my friend, Rhonda, and I got on the wrong train leaving the city and ended up having to get off to switch trains in the heart of Harlem (125th Street.) I was scared then. The only scared feeling I had now was the fear of his family not liking me. I was really nervous about meeting them.

I've met the family of other boyfriends but I was much more self-conscious this time. I wasn't sure they would approve of this white girl their grandson was dating. Maybe I was expecting them to have the same reservations my parents had. His grandparents had a two story Victorian-type home with a porch and all. They greeted me with smiles and made me feel welcome. They were so kind. I was so nervous. I didn't talk much, I let them ask questions. As we visited, I noticed the same friendly personality that attracted me to Joe. I was less nervous as we said our goodbyes, and felt the approval of his grandparents.

My journal:

We walked on the boardwalk at the beach there, hand in hand. We both noticed every one staring but neither one of us cared. It's a really weird feeling because a couple years ago I would've been the one staring and I would think that it was wrong for a black and a white person to be together. I don't even think about him being black until someone comments on it or I see someone looking at us funny.

In June it was time for us to say goodbye, Joe

was going to Jump School at Ft. Benning, Georgia, and I was going back to Arizona to prepare to leave on a mission. We decided to keep in touch and "see what happens." At that point he had told me he loved me, which made me feel good but yet nervous and confused about how I felt. I remember when I got the letter he sent which announced, "I am 100 percent prime time in love." I was flattered but yet uneasy about how fast his feelings were growing for me. So when we parted, I wasn't sure how far I wanted our relationship to go.

CHAPTER 4

Falling

The first night I was back in my home town, I started to miss him. One night, I took a walk, wearing his USMA sweatshirt and my walkman with "our tape" Joe had made. He might as well have been there serenading me. He was Luther, Freddie J and Lionel Richie. During my high school days, I had cruised these streets with my friends, with the goal of meeting up with guys. I smiled and shook my head as I thought of how trivial it seemed now. As the song, "That Night," by Luther came on, my thoughts went back to when we first met, "You see, it actually happened, just like this..." I was really lost in a daydream of Joe when a truck pulled up beside me. I squinted in the darkness before I recognized some old classmates, guys I would have been looking for back in the day. They were the ones looking now, "Ya wanna ride around with us?" I hadn't dated much or gotten too much attention from the boys in high school, so I was flattered by the attention I was getting now. I enjoyed our little chat, bragging that I had been in New York and that I would be going on a mission soon, but I had no desire whatsoever to cruise with them. I wish I would've had this perspective in high school. What a small moment in my life and how insignificant it seemed in comparison with what was in my immediate future. I was glad when they took off. I just wanted to continue being in my own little world with Joe Reed. I couldn't stop thinking about him and wondering when I could see him again.

While I was getting ready for my mission and missing him, Joe was studying the teachings of the church. He took the missionary discussions for the second time and we discussed what he was learning each weekend when he called.

Joe's journal:

7 June 87

I like talking about the Church, I don't know why, but I have this hunger for knowledge about it. I feel guilty sometimes if I don't read something before I go to bed, but sometimes I am just too tired to read.

I have decided to dedicate this summer to growing 1) spiritually 2) physically, 3) intellectually (militarily.) ....."the body is the temple of the soul and mind."

He sent me a watch for my birthday. It was an *Oleg Cassini* with stars on the face that moved with each tick of a second. A note from him said that he wanted me to think of him whenever I looked at it because even with the distance between us, we would be under the same stars and he would always be thinking of me. I didn't let Mom and Dad see the note. They were upset enough about the gift. I kept assuring them that we were just friends and I kept telling myself that we needed to just be friends but my feelings for him were much more than friendly. I knew my parents wouldn't be happy if I told them I was dating Joe. I knew they still had the mindset that it was wrong to date someone of a different race. Dad gave me an inquisitive look when he saw a picture of me with Joe's arms around me, but he didn't say anything. They had to have suspected there was more to our relationship.

I lived with Dennis and Carolyn (my brother and his wife) in Mesa so I could work and save. They put up with our long phone conversations every Sunday and they got used to the many letters showing up in their mailbox. I looked forward to every call, and I daydreamed of dancing with him. Every time I received a letter from him I liked him even more. He thought so deeply about everything that he made me want to learn more about what I believed. He continued to learn about the church as I sent my papers in to go on my mission.

14 June 1987

...here is that cadence I promised to send you.

1ˢᵗ verse -
It's tough to be a Ranger's Wife,
Her man must give his only life.
She looks to the sky and wonders why,
For Freedoms cause that he must die.

Chorus -
O, Hale O, Hale O, Infantry,
Queen of battle Follow me,
The Ranger life's the one for me,
For nothing in this world is free.

2ⁿᵈ verse -
Up in the morning and out of the rack
Greeted at dawn by an early attack;
He looks to the sky and wonders why
For Freedoms cause that he must die.

Chorus

3ʳᵈ verse-
Mortars and artillery;
Scream and burst around me.
I look to the sky and wonder why,
For freedoms cause that I must die.

Chorus

4ᵗʰ verse -
Now here I lie in this Foreign Land,
Bleeding in this foreign sand,
I look to the sky, but have not fear,
My Ranger God is Always near.

From the letter that came with the cadence:

...I am learning more about the church with every word I read, it seems. I am learning so much about things I had questions about. My understanding about things is so much clearer that I know they are true. It feels just great. I can't wait to get back to W. P. (not to study) but to learn more and eventually <u>*join*</u>*!!* ☺

Joe continued to amaze me with how much he was learning, the books he was reading, and the understanding he was gaining. At Jump School he took every moment he could to talk to Mormon cadets. Some were returned missionaries and some were preparing to go on their missions, so they had great discussions about the church. He also looked up missionaries when he was home in order to take the discussions again. An elderly couple, the Hammonds, who taught him, shared with me later that Joe was the one doing the teaching, he had learned so much by then. It was in July when he called and announced he was getting baptized. I was so happy for him and I was happy to have been a part of helping someone through that process even though I don't feel like I did much; he took the ball and ran with it!

Joe's journal:

9 Sept. 1987

I need to catch up on the past two weeks action. On 30 Aug I got baptized in to the Church of Jesus Christ of Latter Day Saints (the Mormons.) The ceremony was beautiful, Elder Garrity baptized me, Mike Lawter gave the gift of the Holy Ghost, and Lisa, Brenda and two other girls sang a musical number for me. It was a truly spiritual experience. The feelings I had then were incredible. I had fasted for 26 hours, so I was kind of hungry, but after receiving the Holy Ghost and being baptized I felt filled with something unusual. I was on a high that I had never felt before. The feeling is indescribable in words; it is just an experience I wish everyone had the chance to have.

That night I called Darla; needless to say she was excited about the whole deal. In my excitement I decided to ask her if she wanted to come out for Labor Day weekend. She blurted out "yes." So we made plans for her to come out on Wednesday and return Monday evening. Her trip out to New York proved to be the best weekend of both our lives.

The plane ride to New York was torture. I was so anxious to see Joe again. My friends, Brenda and Lisa, picked me up and we were on our way in the middle of New York traffic—cab drivers cussing, horns honking, people cutting in front of us. I had a huge smile on my face and I had to yell out, "I'm back!" I loved everything about New York: the skyline, the traffic, the people, the accent, the smells, the food. We drove straight up to West Point, and I loved every mile of green trees which I knew would be changing into brilliant colors soon.

My journal:

When we drove up to Grant Hall where we were to meet him, my stomach was going crazy, doing flips and all sorts of strange things. It was great to see him walking up to me with that big smile on his face! He is so dang cute, all we could do was hug and look at each other and laugh! We both just can't believe we're actually together again.

My feelings had changed for him since I had seen him last. I was now ready to tell him I loved him. I really loved him! I had to wait for the right time though, and that time didn't come for a few days. I don't know why I was nervous to tell him. He had expressed his love for me so many times by then.

Friday night, after we had dinner at my favorite Chinese restaurant in New Rochelle, we went to a park to do our favorite thing—dance! It was a beautiful night, perfect for dancing under the stars. That is when I finally got the nerve to say it; "I love you, Joe!" That was the first time I had said it with such emotion behind it. I had never loved anyone like I loved him.

Joe's journal:

While we danced I sung to her numerous songs that I had memorized from listening to the tape so much. During one of the times I was looking into her eyes she said in an angelic whisper, "I love you!" A feeling of enormous satisfaction came over me, it was the first time a girl had ever said it to me. And she said it with such humble sincerity that all I could say was "I love you too" which I do.

The next day we walked hand in hand all over New York City. We walked through Central Park to get to the Met and the Hard Rock Café. We laughed at the fact that it was such a big deal for us to hold hands. At West Point holding hands is considered "PDA" (public display of affection) which is a "no go." With the exception of Ike Hall, when being escorted by him at West Point, I was only allowed to hold his arm as he held it at a ninety degree angle.

After a long day of walking, it was nice that Joe had thought ahead to make reservations for dinner at a very cozy restaurant called Mama Leone's. We had worked up quite an appetite. After dinner we topped the night off by sharing the best view in the city from the observation deck of the Empire State Building. It was one of those perfect days to file in my memory bank and to bring out during the many days we would spend apart in the future.

Joe's journal:

September 1987

Saying good-bye was easier this time because I knew she really loved me and I her. The last thing I told her was that military life is not all that bad. I guess it was my way of telling her to start thinking about Marriage.

My journal:

My feelings are so confused now. I love him so much and for more than a friend! This weekend I just wanted to

*tell him that I'd come off my mission
and marry him, my feelings are so
strong for him. But I just don't know
what to do, I really don't want to hurt
him but I don't know if I could marry
him. Why do things have to be so
difficult? Why are people prejudiced?
This is so stupid having to worry about
this! My parents are going to have a fit
when I tell them what I've done!*

I don't think I ever told my parents about my little trip. "Why make them worry?" I rationalized.

Joe and I continued to write and call each other as I prepared for my mission.

Letter from Joe: (came with a photo of him in West Point uniform)

Hey Sweetheart   *15 Sept 1987*
                             2:10am

*Today was not a good day, I got
nuked in both mechanics and Electrical
Engineering (juice.) But it's a good day
now because I'm writing to you!* ☺
....Thanks for the cookies/card/letter;

you are the sweetest. My roommate wants me to leave you over to him in my "WILL". I said "no way" she is all mine!

Tonight institute was good as are most church related activities. We discussed Lehi and what he sacrificed to be a Prophet, and Nephi—how he was righteous, and Laman-Lemuel—their wickedness. The class is packed all the time with cadets, Missionaries, Mother's helpers, etc. Some people come a long way for a 50 min. class. But it is teaching me so much I can see why; but then of course you got the girls who are smart (sly) enough to come to institute for the social aspects also (if you catch my drift.)

Now in regards to this picture I have sent you. I guess you should know by now that I am very proud of the uniform I wear and what it and I represent. Not only does it represent the great tradition of West Point, but also its dedication to defend this great land (The Promised Land.) As you know America is the Promised Land and by God's will he has made it possible through the Constitution (legally) and other great works that his Church be established here. Now in order for his Church to prosper he had to put it in a place where it could legally and spiritually prosper. In our times, as we know, the spread of communism is a hindrance to democracy which in turn is a hindrance to the freedom of religion. The armed forces of this country are present to defend the Constitution, Democracy, etc. Now (get ready for this) without the Armed Forces we cannot share in these blessings, if you will, because of the impending presence of communism. In other words, the purpose of the Armed Forces (and this is straight from the General Authorities in Salt Lake) is to defend the Church! ☺

I tell you this because when you look at this picture I want you to see more than just me ☺ O.K.? The responsibility Me, Mike, Frank, Brother Guthrie, and everyone else in uniform has transcends the temporal needs of this world. Although most people do not know this I thought it was time I clued you in on the "Big Picture" of what I do and why....

I think I am going to run in the Marine Corps Marathon in November in Washington D.C. This way I can not only prepare for the possibility of Ranger School, but also visit the Temple and see the flicks (videos) at the Visitor Center. I really can't wait, I have a small picture of the Temple on my desk, because I know the Prophet says we should display one in our home. But also it gives me something to look at when I am pondering spiritual things as I often do.

Well I need to hit the rack soon so I'll write again and talk to ya on Sunday.

Darla, I don't know how to say it, or express it or write it. But I guess that these words can best describe the way I feel!

I'm just - Helplessly in Love with you!

I will Always Love you,

Joe

My journal:

Last week when I got a letter from him and was reading it with a big ear-to-ear grin on my face, Danette was watching on and was curious so I let her read it. The last paragraph he really got serious and said he loved me so much the only way he could really express himself would be to look deep into my eyes down to where my heart resides and say the words of our favorite song, "I'm helplessly in Love with you."! I wondered what she would think of it, I thought she would mock it or something. But I let her read it anyway. After she finished she was crying and she couldn't talk for a while. When she finally gained her composure she said she really felt for the both of us because she knows that we could be deliriously happy with each other but it will be tough because of the parents and everyone else looking down on us.

CHAPTER 5

"Lead Me, Guide Me,
Walk Beside Me,
Help Me Find the Way"
I Pray!
An LDS Hymn by Naomi W. Randall

As I faced my new reality of living my life
without Joe, I knew I had to rely on the Lord like
never before. As I prayed and contemplated where I
should live I tried to imagine the children and myself
in Arizona and in Florida. When I tried to imagine
myself living in Arizona, as much as I loved my family
and knew they wanted to surround me with love and
support, it just didn't feel right. When I pictured us
living by Joe's parents in Florida I felt good. Besides
the positive feeling I had, there were many reasons I
thought it was a good idea to live by my in-laws. They
were grieving as deeply as I was and I knew having

the children close would help the children as well as Joe's parents. I wanted them to help me "keep Joe alive." I thought it was also important that the children be around family who looked like them. These reasons made it easier to follow through with moving my little family across the country. The main force behind my move though, was the feeling that I had in my chest every time I thought about it, talked about it, and prayed about it. It was unmistakably where the Lord wanted me to be.

I'm grateful for those strong feelings, because it wasn't easy telling my mother what I had decided. She didn't like me going so far away because she wanted to be there for me and help me through this difficult time.

I'd written in a journal since 8th grade and had always written as if talking to an anonymous friend, but now, after Joe died, I wrote most of my entries to him, my best friend.

My journal:

Dear Joe,   *June 1996*

I found out today that our baby inside me is a girl, her name will be Jessica. Having a new baby in my life hasn't sunk in as I am so overwhelmed with your absence. It has helped to be with my parents; Mom keeps me well fed and off my feet and Dad plays with JR and Jasmine. I know they would do anything to take my pain away. I have made a decision; I have been praying to know where I should live, and I believe I have gotten an answer. After the baby is born I will move close to your parents; it's been hard for mom to understand but I can only imagine my life there with your family, I know it will be best...for all of us. We need each other right now; I know they are the only ones who are missing you as much as I am.

I will always love you,
Darla

Our third child was born on June 26, 1996. Jessica was breech so I was scheduled to deliver her at 8:00 in the morning, but just like my other children, she was anxious to get here. I started going into labor during the night and knew I wasn't going to be able to wait till 8:00, so I showed up to the hospital at 6:00. The doctors and nurses were moving slowly as if they were still going to stick with the schedule, so I had to give them the 411 on how fast my other babies came. I wasn't going to deal with hard labor as well as a c-section, thank you very much! After they examined me, they all started moving at a more appropriate pace! My father kept J.R. and Jasmine occupied in the waiting room, while my mom and mother-in-law came in to support me. I was a little relieved to have both of them there, but I still felt very alone and anxious without Joe. My mind was still filled with the question of how the heck the Lord expected me to raise three children by myself when the doctor announced I had given birth to a healthy baby girl. "Ready or not," I thought. I smiled as my mother-in-law held her new grandchild up and presented her to God just like Kunta Kinte in *Roots*.

What a gift from heaven! I knew Joe had just held her and must have had quite a chat with her. I imagined a military type briefing on what she should expect and advice on choices she should make. I was hoping he had told her to sleep through the night for her mommy. He might have, but she didn't seem to remember because she was just like our other two babies—up every couple hours. I had multiple chats with God about how unfair this was, but as tired and overwhelmed as I was, I still enjoyed holding and gazing at this little one who had inherited so many characteristics from her father.

That summer we had two other additions to our extended family. My sister-in-law, Carolyn, had a baby in July, and Danette had a baby in August. We decided that it would be nice to have all three babies blessed on the same day. I liked this idea so I planned my move in September. I asked my brother, Dale, to bless her for me. It broke my heart to think of anyone but Joe, who had blessed J.R. and Jasmine, doing it, but I thought it would be a little easier to be surrounded by family on that difficult day. I read Joe's last journal entry over and over again, the one where he recounted the moment he gave Jasmine her blessing.

31 January 1995

The spirit of the Lord flowed much more freely as I blessed my first daughter in church on Sunday. Grandma Cathcart and Danette Matthews, Darla's mother and sister have come to visit for a few days, so Bishop Ribera let us bless Jasmine on a day other than Fast Sunday. The men that participated in the blessing included Bishop John Ribera, Allan Krausz, Bill Winn, Doug Chipman, and Jon Bulseco. I was concerned while the blessing was being given that I wasn't putting all of my words together properly, but then the spirit flowed more freely as I blessed her with her most divine calling in this life; "to marry in the temple to a young man who has been raised in the Gospel who will honor his priesthood, to follow her mother and grandmother's example in bringing forth children and teaching them the things that will bring them home to Heavenly Father.

September came and with it, our move to Florida. My father flew with us, as he had done as we left North Carolina to go to Arizona. He was my quiet hero. He helped me sell my house, and care for the kids, and he jumped in and did whatever he could do to lighten my load. All summer, he took J.R. everywhere he went, and he was Jasmine's horsey whenever she requested it.

While living with my parents, I thought a lot about who my dad was. As I reflected, something that had happened a couple years previous was more significant to me now. My extended family threw a big party for my grandmother when she turned 80 years old (I was pregnant with Jasmine at the time.) Throughout the day, two of my uncles were telling jokes and stories and being "the life of the party." When it was time to eat, one of my uncles asked my father to offer the blessing on the food. My father obliged and he offered thanks to God for family and for all of the blessings that we enjoy. It was a lengthy prayer. When he finished, this same uncle said, "Dang Ed, we can't ever get you to talk, but when you pray, we can't get you to shut up!" That got a laugh from most, but I just stared at my father and thought about what was said. Yes, my dad was the quiet type. But through the years, I've heard too many stories of charismatic men making horrible decisions that have left their families devastated. I was grateful to know that my dad would always love Mom, and always love us, and always make decisions based on his faith and his love for us. As a child, I didn't value that quality in him, but right then, I couldn't have been more proud to say, "That's my dad!"

Dropping us off in Florida had to be hard for Dad, knowing he wouldn't see us for a while. I wished I would have hugged him harder and thanked him more sincerely. My mother-in-law said she was touched as she watched him say goodbye to the children. She saw that it was difficult for him but he had a look of resolve.

I anticipated the difficulty of this transition but I never imagined how hard it would be to live in a place that brought up so many memories. Joe and I had visited his parents many times through the years, and every time we visited, we tried different restaurants, dance clubs, and of course, Disney World. It seemed that every corner I turned, I had flash backs of moments with Joe. He was so determined to have me know the area. While he drove he would explain how Orlando was set up and how Colonial Drive ran east and west and how it met Orange Blossom Trail. I would nod my head and say, "uh huh," with no real desire to remember anything he said. He would always be driving anyway. We also drove around looking at houses, picking out the ones we liked. We talked of someday living here, maybe as he retired from the military. As the memories flooded my mind, I prayed that he would be able to help me find the right home for us now. I wasn't ready to do it alone.

My journal:

> *Dear Joe*   *September 1996*
>
> *We're here in Orlando now. J.R. just went to his first day of preschool, I thought of you and wished you were there to share my excitement....He's adjusting pretty well, but I know there are hard times ahead as he more fully understands how definite his separation from you is. Joe, it is really hard to accept this, he needs his daddy. What are you doing that is so much more important? It doesn't get any easier as the days pass. J.R. misses his daddy and so do I.*

After church today as I drove past the cemetery I hesitated and then decided to go ahead and go in. I thought I could find the place where your body is buried. As I searched the grounds I became upset and started crying, I couldn't find you. I've looked for you many times Joe; in Malls and other places where we've gotten separated, but now I was looking for you at a cemetery! The reality of that was too much for me and I wept at the thought. I miss you sweetheart and it hurts more and more as the numbness wears off and reality sinks in. My whole life without you babes, I still want to ask why, even though I think I know some of the reasons, goodnight babes, I love you.

As I struggled to fathom my husband's death and my new life without him, my little boy was also trying to comprehend what had happened. One day when he was with his Aunt Vonda he told her that he missed his daddy, "He used to play with me." He then added, "Now Daddy is in heaven playing with Jesus."

It took a while for J.R. to like preschool, I would

stay until his first recess sometimes, but the longer I stayed the more he would protest as I left. He would break my heart with, "Don't do this to me Mommy! Don't leave me!" I couldn't handle his dramatic pleas. I called Victoria, my Willcox therapist, for advice. She told me that each day before I dropped him off, I needed to assure him I would be back and that he would be fine, and then I needed to hand him to the teacher and leave. Consistency would help him to see it would be all right. I needed to say the same things and do everything the same way, every day. If I stayed with him, I would validate his idea that school was a scary place where he needed his mommy close by. After three days of this ritual, as we drove to the preschool, he asked, "Do I have to go to school today?"

"Yes." I answered.

"Are you going to leave me with my teacher?"

"Yes, I am, but you'll be fine and I'll pick you up after lunch, just like yesterday."

He slumped in his seat and said, "Well, what can I do?"

He laid his head on the teachers shoulder this time and gave in as I walked away. He didn't cry that day so I cried for him. J.R. improved everyday to the point where he looked forward to going to school, thanks to Victoria!

I closed on my new home in November of that year. It was bigger than I thought I should have, but I felt good about the neighborhood and I loved the pillars that were on each side of the double door entry way. My big home and the pillars brought me a little happiness. I thought of it as my consolation prize—a gift from Joe.

The excitement of the home melted away as all of our "goods" were delivered. Joe's things had been in storage all this time. As I unpacked them I cried, stopping and remembering a special moment attached to every object. Since the master bathroom had two closets, I designated one of them to be Joe's. I hung his clothes on the racks and hung his pictures, awards, certificates, and hats on the walls. On the lower shelves, I put his favorite books, his medals, his dog tags, his cologne, his brush, and his hair gel. On the higher shelves I arranged his Sunday shoes, his military boots, his West Point hat with the plume in it, and his church briefcase given to him by his friend, Kevin. This closet was his space. I would go in and touch his things and remember and cry. I would open his Sportin' Waves hair gel, which still had his finger imprints in it from the last time he had used it. I would sit on the floor with it under my nose, breathe in deeply, and take in that familiar scent.

As I went through box after box, my anticipation

mounted for the moment I would find Joe's letters he had written to me. I had saved them all, from the first one after we met to the last one he sent me while he was serving in Desert Storm. When I opened the right box revealing my treasure; a box full of letters from my sweetheart, I burst into tears! I pulled a card out first, one of the many he sent me while we were long distance dating. The title alone brought another flood of emotion. How could something he sent me so long ago speak to my heart right now?

While We're Apart

It's not easy for us while distance
Separates us.
As each day passes into another,
We must look forward to tomorrow,
Knowing that we are one day closer
To the dreams we hold.
It may be frustrating when we need
A hug or want each other's
Company.
If we feel alone, we should close
Our eyes
And remember a moment in time
When we held one another…
Remember our smiles,
And listen to our warm voices,

And feel the love that surrounds us.
We must live each day together,
Even though distance keeps us apart.
Let's live each day, side by side –
Let's feel comfortable with our love,
For then our loneliness will leave us.
Missing each other will help us
Gain confidence in our togetherness,
And we'll grow while we're apart.

-Anne Marie Holleran

What he wrote in the card:

June of '87

Darla,

As I sit here next to you, I wonder how long we will last. Yesterday was the greatest, and I want it to last forever. (Maybe it can) Anyway this card should sum things up pretty well. I really want us to grow together while we're apart and teach each other as we have been doing for the past 3 months. No matter what happens there is now and ALWAYS will be a place in my heart for you, Darla.

Loving you, Always and Forever,

Joe

I put the box of letters in his closet so I could be surrounded with his belongings as I read them. These were more precious to me than anything else in that closet. I was amazed with this blessing of having such a big part of him preserved. I was also amazed with how significant his words felt to me now. I read them as if he were communicating with me again. They felt like letters straight from heaven.

CHAPTER 6

"Called to Serve"
An LDS Hymn by Grace Gordan

We continued to live at my in-laws home while I unpacked our belongings and made arrangements for blinds. Sometimes Mamie would watch the kids so I could get more done. Sometimes I would get more done, but sometimes I would sit in his closet, with my box of letters and pull them out randomly and read and remember and cry. I liked to hold my head up with my eyes closed and pull out an envelope from the bottom of the box like I was pulling out the name of a grand prize winner.

> *O, d'être une l'arme*
> *De naître dans ton oeil*
> *De vivre sur ta joue*
> *Et de mourir sur tes lèvres.*

The poem in the middle of the letter jumped out at me, and I started sobbing. This poem was so much more meaningful now, how could he have gotten it so right? At the time, I was just impressed that he sent me a French poem. I closed my eyes and traveled back to the time he sent it, back to the Mission Training Center. I ran, with the letter in hand, trying desperately to find the French girl I had met, to translate for me, with my other new friends running behind.

As soon as I spotted her I pushed the letter into her hands begging her to tell me what it said. As she read, she sighed, with her hand on her chest and said something in French.

She really had me going. I was jumping up and down by then, "Tell me, tell me!" As she struggled with her English, she slowly revealed to us the English version.

Oh to be a tear
To be born in your eye
To live on your cheek
And to die on your lips.

My new friends all sighed loudly with me, "Now

you know why I love him!" I bragged.

As I remembered that moment I shook my head and cried and smiled. "You truly are in the tears I cry Joe, you had no idea how many tears I'd cry for you did you?"

I skimmed the letter, searching for more significant words from my husband, and then I rummaged through the envelopes again, pulling out another. Ah, October '87, when I left on my mission, the ending of our ability to call each other.

Yes on Sunday I was a "hurtin' unit." It made me realize how much of a friend you really are to me. Monday I felt like I lost my right arm (you) so now I'm learning how to use the left. When you get back can I have my arm back? ☺

I thought to myself, Monday...the day I found out...the day I lost my right arm...I want it back...I don't want to learn how to use my left.

My mind went back to my mission, I was so happy then. I remembered the joy I felt when I found out where I was going to serve. My parents received the letter and then started trying to track me down. This was before cell phones were in everyone's hand, only the rich-enough had them. They actually opened the envelope without me and knew before I did! Before I had time to get upset, they blurted out "Switzerland, French speaking!!"

"Woo hoo!" I couldn't stop smiling.

A couple months later, I said goodbye to my family and friends and flew to Provo, Utah. I stayed with my Aunt Uni and Uncle Marvin a couple days before I was scheduled to enter into the Mission Training Center (MTC) so I could have a chance to buy some cold weather clothes. They also took me to Salt Lake City to go through the temple there and tour Temple Square. The Christus was inspiring, I looked at this majestic statue and thought of how I would now be working for Him. I could sense His love for me and His love and concern for the world. As my aunt and uncle dropped me off at the M.T.C., I felt the responsibility of my new job and was anxious to get started. There was a short orientation, a goodbye moment with our families, and we were introduced to our MTC companions. We had to be with our companion 24-7 and I hit the jackpot with Sharla Cardon! Sharla and Darla: we were both from

Arizona, we both struggled with French, and we both loved to laugh. We had to memorize the first discussion in French. I hardly knew what I was saying as I would spout out what sounded like: "Lay plupart day jon cwa donsune Etra Souprem ..." ("Most people believe in a Supreme Being...")   I was humbled like I'd never been humbled before. I was slapped in the face with the reality that after two years of French at Eastern Arizona College (EAC), I still couldn't communicate in this language. We had covered everything I knew by the second day! And after a lifetime of being a member of the Church, I had no idea how to present my beliefs to others! I started to realize that with Joe but the MTC humbled me even more. I gained a strong desire to learn, to improve, to grow, and to be the kind of missionary God needed me to be.

It was like going from French class to church all day, every day, for two months. I was able to hear inspirational talks by some of my favorite people, including George Durrant and Mary Ellen Edmonds. They helped me feel good about who I was and what I was doing and they inspired me to be better. They were also extremely funny.

We were also privileged to go to a BYU devotional where we listened to the prophet speak. I had his signature on my mission call, President Ezra Taft Benson. I had been honored to hear him speak in person once before. It was in New York, when I was a nanny. As a church group we went to the Hill Cumorah Pageant, close to Palmyra. I was already amazed with having our Sunday meeting on the Hill Cumorah, where Joseph Smith found the gold plates. I was pretty close to the pulpit, sitting on a blanket when there was an announcement made. It was President Benson's birthday and he had paid us a surprise visit! He walked right by me as he went to the pulpit. I remember seeing this humble man smile at us and I remember feeling my heart burn as he spoke. He was the prophet on the earth. I felt it deep within me that day. When I saw him at BYU with thousands of other missionaries and BYU students in the big dome, I felt fortunate to have been so close to him back in New York, but I still had the same feeling that I had back on the hill. A prophet of God was speaking to me. I knew it and I listened intently. He spoke to us about staying morally clean and how to repent if we have already fallen into sin. As he and his wife stopped to wave at us on their way out, I thought of the fact that I was working for him as well as the Lord. What a blessing to have had such loving bosses!

The MTC was a great place to be. It was good to be a bit sheltered from the world and to be able to focus on my faith. Joe kept the letters coming, always with a dose of encouragement and advice.

The missionary like the warrior must never let his spirit be broken! If he falls seven times, he must get up eight times!

(Author unknown)

Remember that I will always love you and that I have faith in you. Drive on Ranger!

20 Oct. 1987
(11:45 pm)

Oh guess what? I was asked to give a Fireside to the young men and young women. I think they want to hear how I found the church and all the troubles and trials I went through and kind of still am. I have been approached before about talking about it. Ya know I can think of nothing better to do than strengthening young kid's testimonies by sharing my experiences, because I know by strengthening theirs I will strengthen my own. After all that is what church conferences, gatherings, meetings, etc are for, to bring the people together to strengthen each other by sharing their testimonies.

We always received our mail while in the lunch line. The district leader would go get the mail and then hand it out. This made getting mail even more essential. Just imagine everyone's name being called out except yours. Between my family and friends and Joe, there weren't too many no-mail days for me.

3 Nov. 1987

The Stripling Warriors are my kinda guys. I can see how I want to be, in them. Alma 53: 18-21

The stripling warriors are a group of young men, mentioned in the Book of Mormon, who volunteer to go to war. They are ready to fight for their religion and freedom. They had great faith as they stepped forward to battle, knowing the Lord was with them.

The reference Joe gave reads:

Now behold, there were two thousand of those young men, who entered into this covenant and took their weapons of war to defend their country.

And now behold, as they never had hitherto been a disadvantage to the Nephites, they became now at this period of time also a great support; for they took their weapons of war, and they would that Helaman should be their leader.

And they were all young men, and they were exceedingly valiant for courage, and also for strength and activity; but behold, this was not all—they were men who were true at all times in whatsoever thing they were entrusted.

Yea, they were men of truth and soberness, for they had been taught to keep the commandments of God and to walk uprightly before him. Alma 53: 18-21 Book of Mormon

While I was trying to learn French and preparing myself to teach the gospel, Joe was having amazing experiences at West Point.

Dec '87

...President Reagan's speech was inspiring. It was nice being a part of U.S. history in the making. We were on all the television stations and in every Newspaper across the country."

"Saturday we went to the Bi-Regional dance. We were mauled as soon as we stepped in the door. Needless to say the place was packed with desperate Nanny's. ... Although I had fun... I must tell you that every dance I was thinking of you and how much better it would be with you. With you it is not dancing, it is floating away to another planet moving to a beat that only our hearts when together can make.—(Now you gotta give me credit that was a pretty good one, don't you think?) ☺

I couldn't believe I was going to fly to Switzerland. It was almost too much excitement for this little small town girl to handle. Cardon and I made a face at each other as we prepared for take off. It was called the fright face. Cardon was the queen of faces. She had one for every occasion, and this moment was definitely a fright face moment. You have to tighten up your whole face, bug your eyes, and let your mouth drop. It expressed perfectly our mixed emotions of excitement and fear and anxiety. My first moment of trying to speak French in public was on the two story plane to Geneva. I tried to ask where the bathroom was. The flight attendant was not in a good mood! As soon as I started stuttering out my practiced phrase, "Ou se trouve le salle de bain?" she cut me off and said, "What do you want?"

"Ok fine, I'll speak English, bust my little bubble why don't you!" This was the introduction to many humbling moments as I struggled to learn another language.

I entered the Geneva Airport in a daze, my eyes widened as I heard the announcements in French, *"Oh my! Darla, you're not in Willcox anymore!"* The mission president, his wife and a couple missionaries came toward us with hands stretched out to shake ours. "Bienvenue!" They were all smiles and made me feel a little at ease. I was still in a daze as we toted our suitcases out of the airport and loaded them into a van.

My first experience outside the airport was at a food court. I was expected to order for myself—in French! I stared blankly at the woman ready to take my order. I guessed that she had asked me what I would like to order but I didn't understand a word! She spoke so fast! *"What have I gotten myself into?"* kept running through my mind.

That night I had an interview with President Hassell. He asked me what he should know about me. I let him know that I was from Arizona and that I hated being cold. The next day I was on train to the coldest city in the mission, Dijon, France. *Thanks Pres.*

Dear Darla   *Dec 9. 1987*

...We had two baptisms this week. ....It brought back memories. Mark had a glow and look in his eye a person can only have when they are perfectly clean. I needed a spiritual experience this week. There is so much that goes on around here that can tempt or lead a person astray that it is difficult to stay close to Heavenly Father, and keep the commandments.

You know Darla it is so wonderful to finally know the Truth after all these years. Do you remember when we would talk about church ....and do you remember how I would always say I was so confused about things? Well I know now what was happening. Heavenly Father was preparing me for what was to come. I was supposed to be confused so that I would seek the answers, and finally - finally get the Truth, something that I always wanted and needed. And there are others who need it just as I did. That my friend is where you come in......so go forth and teach. ☺"

My toes froze that first day. Sister Broom, my new companion, was nice enough to put "buy boots" on our schedule for the next day. Soeur (French for "sister," sounds like "sir") Broom was American but had been a missionary for a while. She spoke French fluently and was experienced. I sat quietly and listened when we went to visit people. I struggled to understand, and I struggled to speak. It was a slowwww difficult road, but I was determined to keep moving forward.

Even saying "Bonjour" was not as easy as I thought. People on the street would respond with "'Scuzez moi?" (Excuse me?) And then I would attempt to say it again and again until they either ran away or got what I was trying to pronounce. I felt like a two year old, quite humbling!

Dearest Darla,   *Dec 20. 1987*

...Right now I'm sitting on my plane, waiting to go home. Term Ends went OK I guess, you never can tell. Damon Owens, a plebe [freshman], was waiting with me at my gate, his flight left at 8:05 pm so he had to wait awhile. I forgot to tell you about him he is both a brother, and one of the brethren, like me. ☺ Get the drift, I knew you would.

95

He is so funny, he is always complaining about being a plebe when we go on LDS trips.

Last night 'The Sound of Music' was on in the Dayroom. I never realized how bad some people can distort something so innocent into porn. I tried to watch it with guys in the company, but they were just terrible. I started to get upset so they all took a pill. Anyway, the movie reminded me of my favorite Nanny! Who could that be, I wonder! Well I'm gonna read some of Talmage, 'Articles of Faith' ...Chow!

Christmas Eve in Dijon was memorable. We ate a meal I thought would never end. A nice family, members of the church there, invited six of us missionaries over. Everything we ate was brought out separately, if I had known how many entrees there were, I would have eaten smaller proportions. The hors d'oeuvre was bread with pate, cheese and eggs. Next, some shrimp and salmon and stuffed tomatoes were served. I thought this was the main dish but it wasn't. The main dish was turkey and chestnuts followed by asparagus, and then to finish the meal we had more bread with fruit and seven different types of cheese. I was stuffed, but wait, there's dessert, an ice cream cake I just had to try! Oh lo lo! (Oh my!)

I was glad we had to walk to where we were going next because I was about to bust open. We had plans to attend a midnight mass in the Saint-Benigne Cathedral. I remember wanting to preserve this moment: the sound of our shoes on the cobble stone, the crisp air, the fog setting in, the sound of the bells of the cathedral in the distance, getting louder as we walked towards them. The little small town girl in me wanted to run and scream, "Wow! Look where I am, this is incredible!!" Instead I breathed deep and closed my eyes for a while to take it all in. The cathedral was dark and cold. We sat in wooden chairs that were set up in rows, filling the open space. I scanned the area as I tried to understand the Christmas message, which was in Latin. The priest was standing in a raised circular stand on the left side of the pillar lined chapel. There was a pipe organ that reminded me of the Mormon Tabernacle organ in Salt Lake City, Utah, with the huge pipes exposed. With so much being foreign to me, I was grateful for the one universal song I recognized and was happy to join in as we all sang, "Douce Nuit" ("Silent Night".)

Hi Darla,   *5 Jan 88*

...The Church has definitely taught me how important family is and I loved

them more than ever this trip ...but ...My parents are embarrassed and they don't tell anyone that I am Mormon. I didn't make a fuss about it, I wanted to be happy and have a good visit this time. So I chilled out. I managed to get to church a few times, went to a Fireside and even fellowshipped members and missionaries.

But I also went to church with my family. I said Hi to everyone and they all smothered me with praises about W.P. and how tall & straight I am etc. This is where things got mixed up. I realized these people love me and they expect me to do a lot. I felt like I let them down, but by the same token I know what I have done (am doing) is right. It is my unavoidable destiny that must fulfill a plan, devised before I was born.

Something you learn to deal with on a mission is change. After a couple months, I received a new companion. This meant it was up to me to know which bus to take and to keep our list of addresses and people straight. Soeur Rougier and I got lost quite a bit. I am grateful she was patient and forgiving.

We would be riding one bus and I would point to a bus passing us going the opposite direction while saying, "I think we're supposed to be on that bus right there!"

Besides learning how to get around in Dijon, I also learned lessons that would help me to look beyond myself and my problems. I came to the conclusion that driving a station wagon in high school could no longer be classified as a serious trial or hardship, even when it has wooden panels. In Dijon I met many refugees who would've been killed if they'd stayed in their home countries. All of the challenges I'd faced in my life seemed trivial in comparison.

One couple we were teaching lived in a small studio apartment, about 15ft x 15ft. They had a bed, a small kitchenette, and a community toilet down an outside walkway. They bathed in a small washtub that they had to fill with water from the sink, which was heated, a pot at a time, on their stove. They were so grateful for this "beautiful, safe home." I began to feel very rich, and ashamed for ever thinking of myself as poor.

With more responsibility, I was forced to do more speaking. I talked to people in the streets, on the bus, in the park, in their homes, and tried to share with them how Jesus Christ could change their lives and my French was actually good enough to be understood! I remember having a strong love for people, a genuine concern for total strangers. I prayed to know how I could touch their hearts and help them to want more. I loved to get the Book of Mormon into their hands especially after the prophet, President Benson, had admonished us to "flood the earth with the Book of Mormon."

My ability to communicate in French improved, although I continued to be humbled. A small girl I was talking to in my best French, turned to her mother and asked, "Pourquoi me parles-t-elle dans l'anglais? Je ne comprens pas d'anglais!" (Why is she talking to me in English? I don't understand English!) *"Quelle Haunt!" (How embarrassing)*

We did have many disappointments and difficult moments: riding a bike in a dress in the rain, people "biffing" us (no shows) all day long, one of us sick in bed, people slamming the door in our face. One time I slid down the middle aisle of the bus, wet from the rain, like I was sliding into home base, this while still holding onto our groceries from the *supermarche*. Some days, when we were really discouraged, we would joke about taking the *TGV* to Paris. We could be there in about ninety minutes on that train.

We received plenty of, "Ca ne m'interest pas" (that doesn't interest me.) I wanted to ask "If you were on your death bed, would you be interested then?" There were many others who wanted to listen and who changed their lives as we taught them. Some had the desire to be baptized and that gave me a feeling of joy that I had only felt once before (when Joe was baptized.) Another great lesson I learned: being in the service of others really can give you an indescribable joy. I was so happy sometimes I felt like skipping and singing as we went from one visit to the next.

My Dear Darla,   *20 Jan. 1988*
(and still trippen' over you)

...Well this Sunday I get ordained.... It still amazes me that I can hold the 'Holy Priesthood'. Some people may take this for granted but this is serious stuff. Maybe I'm too hard on myself, but why would I be called, as unworthy a soul as I am. Suddenly this idea of being 'perfect' is for real. Because I will be asked to give blessings, ordain others etc., therefore not only do I owe it to myself to be spotless but to those who ask me to perform these ordinances. (Especially my family.) The weight of this responsibility is growing everyday for me. Heck Darla, last year at this time I not only had no idea of the church but I never dreamed of being a Priest and much less an Elder.... There

are guys that knew this was coming all their lives and prepared. Here I am fresh off the block.

But then again as I reflect on a life time of experiences, I was being prepared with out knowledge of it. Heavenly Father definitely has a plan.......And, my friend, I'm afraid the plan has a lot left to unfold! I guess we'll have to wait and see what's coming up next. I love you Darla!

All of my companions heard about Joe and they listened and gave their opinion as I debated on the possibility of us being married some day. I would sometimes think that I could never marry him—my parents would freak! But then I would receive a letter and I would think, "Let them freak, this guy is too amazing!" We sent a few tapes to one another too. It seemed he was learning about the doctrines of the church as fast as I was. He continued to inspire me with his understanding of the scriptures and his willingness to follow every guideline he was taught.

Letter from Joe:

...I know the church is true and have

belief & faith, but there is more to it.

Before when I spoke of knowledge – I have a great knowledge that is building every day. I've learned more about the gospel in 4 months than most people do in a whole year. And I did it on top of all my West Point requirements. But there is a difference between knowledge & wisdom and belief & Faith. This is something I talked over with Dennis on the phone as well as reading in Talmage. –

"Belief is in a sense passive, an agreement or acceptance only; faith is active and positive embracing such reliance and confidence as will lead to works.

Yet he may believe and still lack faith. Faith is vivified, vitalized living belief. If belief be a product of the mind, faith is of the heart: belief is founded on reason, faith largely on intuition, and finally, knowledge. –

Knowledge is to wisdom what belief is to faith, one an abstract principle, the other a _living application_."

After five months in Dijon, I was transferred to Marignane, just north of Marseille, France. My new companion, Soeur Lawler couldn't have been more different from me. I still remember our first conversation:

"Do you like sports?"

"No, I like solving physic equations and playing Dungeons and Dragons."

"Hmm."

Surprisingly, we were a great team. I told stories and shared feelings and she knew where every scripture was and remembered needed details during our discussions. Another lesson learned – different personalities shouldn't be looked at as an obstacle, but as an asset. We got along just great, regardless of how different our interests were.

Almost everyone in that village had rose gardens and they were all in bloom. I had never seen roses so big and in such a variety of colors. The dogs were big too. Almost every home had a big dog out in front of their home. Thankfully, their yards were all enclosed in iron rod fencing with a locked gate in front. But their big dog started barking like crazy as soon as we rang the bell at the gate. The home owner would emerge and usually stay on their porch as they asked what we wanted. We would then have to yell our invitation for them to listen to a message about Christ, and they would yell back with their "No merci" or "Ca ne m'interest pas," or my favorite, "Less moi tranquille" (leave me tranquil.) Not my favorite way to talk to people!

I was there for only one month when I was transferred to Yverdon, Switzerland. Green, quaint, friendly, plenty of chocolate, cheese, and patisseries— who wouldn't want to live here? I absolutely loved being able to walk to the market, and bike to other villages which surrounded Lake Neufchatel. And let's not forget the castle in the center of every village. My new companion, Soeur Arrieus humbled me a little more. She was French and took it upon herself to improve my vocabulary and accent. It was painfully necessary!

The debate about Joe still played in my head and with my companion when there was down time, especially when I got a letter from him. I was honest about my reservations. I just didn't know how it would all work out between us.

21 Feb. '88

...The one thing that I really want to talk to you about is about us! ☺ *I too wonder everyday if things will work out between us when you return. I think*

about everything you think about too, everyday. And when I analyze 'the Situation' (as you nicely put it) I see more good than bad, in other words, the Pros outweigh the Cons. And although it will be hard, especially dealing with our parents, I know we'll work through it together. I'm 22 today and if I can't make a decision on my own about how I want to live _my_ life, and who I want to spend it with then I'm a hurtin' unit, and so are you. Besides I never asked for anything to be easy, just fair. You know as well as I, nothing worthwhile or lasting comes easy to anyone. Maybe, just maybe this is our test. All I know is that I love you dearly and what I want most is to make you happy. And even though I know that I could bring you that happiness despite the cost, I would give you up if it meant you would be happier without me. It would be more painful than anything I've ever done, but I'd do it nonetheless because I love you! Now I know this is a lot, but I thought you wanted to know how I really felt about "The Situation."

Oh yeah! There is a new song out by a new singer named Rick Ashley. This *guy looks like "Opey" on the Andy Griffith Show, but he sounds like Nat King Cole. Anyway I like the words to it; it's called "When I Fall in Love."*

"When I fall in love it will be forever,
Or I'll never fall in love;
When I give my heart it will be completely
Or I'll never give my heart.
And the moment that I feel that you
Feel that way too- is when I
Fall in love with you."

Yes I know it is short but it says it all.
☺ I love you.

While I was in Switzerland, Joe was sent to Germany for some training, not far from where I was. Instead of just showing up at my door, he called the mission president to see if he could call me on my birthday. They had a great conversation about West Point and the gospel, but President Hassell didn't give him permission to call me, and so he didn't.

Dear Darla,   *(Summer '88)*

Guess where I am right now? I'm on the plane to Europe!!... Tell your comp if I can get some butterfingers here I'll send them, however, if I send some you both had better go running or at least do something extremely physical. (No fat Sisters allowed!) I will not contribute to an unhealthy cause, unless it involves "chocolate chip cookies", they are the only exception to the rule.

My companion and I did like to run, and we walked everywhere we went, but we also had a woman in our branch (small congregation) who lived above a patisserie. She would call us to help her eat the pastries she had been given at the end of the day—a tray full of strawberry tarts, croissants, pains au chocolats, mille fuilles, and beignets. I wanted one of each! Joe would not have approved!

Visit home after his Internship in Germany:

Dear Darla,   *(Summer '88)*

....Also yesterday while at home my mom had me watch a '60's movie called 'Guess Who's Coming to Dinner' starring Spencer Tracy, Katharine Hepburn and

Sidney Poitier. It was about a Black man & white girl who fell in love and were planning to get married, however, they were seeking the parents' blessings.

The movie was great and had a 'Happy' ending. Many things were said in it that our parents should hear, and I'm glad mine did. They said that it really caused an uproar in the early 60's, but it was also nominated for an Academy Award along with the actors & actresses. But instead of me it affected them the most, because this morning on our way to church Mom asked about your parents and what they thought of the 'situation!' I really did not know what to say so I said 'I don't know' cuz I don't. Anyway she really doesn't mind, she just wonders about you! And if that's all she worries about, then I'm relieved because you're the greatest thing since 'sliced bread!' (Oh and choc. Chip cookies too) I just thought you'd like an update on the home 'situation!'

Do you know what I just thought of? One month from today I go through the Temple! ☺ Isn't that something? And in 27 days it will be my one year

Baptismal anniversary. Yaaay! Time sure has flown by quickly.

Soeur Arrieus's tutoring prepared me for my next experience—having a sixteen year old French girl as a companion. Soeur Blareau loved to talk, usually 100 kilometers per hour and not a bit of it in English. I appreciated that she sacrificed a month of her summer to give me an advanced French lesson while simultaneously serving others. Just when I was gaining so much confidence from this experience, a woman I spoke to on the streets responded with, "Je suis desole, je ne parle pas Allemande!" (I'm sorry I don't speak German.) Humble pie was my favorite—I had, by now, acquired a taste for it.

Aug. 88

...It all began Friday at 1650 in front of the barracks when we had a formation in our 'Beast' company. (That's the company we began in when we first arrived here at W.P.) Then we went into the Mess Hall for the Ring Ceremony and Dining-in. I always wondered what happened when the Firsties disappeared into the mess hall. There we had an Invocation followed by a series of toasts (Grape juice for me

T.Y.V.M) [thank you very much] Then General Fred Gordon made a few comments and then finally we had the ring presentation and donned our rings.

Darla I just couldn't put it on; I just wanted to look at it and admire it. After we compared rings, dinner was served, we had Filet Mignon, and Lobster Tail...

Darla it was a magnificent sight! We were all in India whites wearing red sashes, whew! What a beautiful occasion... After the reception we went into the Mess Hall to prepare for seating. But before I went in I had to check my mail! ☺ And much to my surprise was a letter from my Date!! You! So I was walking around reading your letter while all these officers, cadets & dates are engaging in small talk. So when everyone asked me where my date was I showed them the letter. Capt. Guthrie took a picture of me & your letter on Washington Statue.

Darla I can't wait until Graduation so you and I can go to it arm in arm (hand in hand☺) People ask about you constantly, heck you're a legend! But *seriously Darla, this weekend was great and I wanted so much to share it with you. I also wish I could share this next weekend with you. This one is millions more important than Ring Weekend. I just want you to know that I really do love you and there's not a moment that goes by when you aren't somewhere in my thoughts.*

Joe went through the temple one year after he was baptized (the weekend that was "millions more important"). The closest temple was in Washington DC, and as president of the LDS Institute, Joe planned many temple trips.

In October of 1988 (I'd been on my mission for a year at this point) I received a very disturbing letter from my parents telling me that they had gotten an early morning call (6:00 AM) from someone first asking them if they knew their daughter was dating a black boy and then letting them know that they did not like it. They said they were friends of the Reeds. They knew how upset the Reeds were about our relationship and they wanted to make my parents aware of the situation. My parents really don't *do* drama like this. They were very upset by this call. I thought it was a little crazy. For crying out loud, we hadn't physically seen each other for over a year! I was getting used to being in Europe where race didn't seem to be such a huge issue. Joe said his family was more upset about his change of religion than our difference of race. He said that their reservations about me were more so concerning me being the one associated with his change of religion.

I hadn't kept my parents up to date on my feelings for Joe. The idea of us ever dating hadn't been verbalized even though they most likely knew we were more than friends. I wrote them a letter back and was a little more honest with them. I let them know that I loved Joe very much and I tried to explain what an amazing person he was. But I also asked them to not worry about it because we didn't have any plans for now.

I also let Joe know about the call and he responded:

...Frankly I could care less what other people think about us, that is their problem, not ours. And although the ideal relationship would include our parents blessing, the decision and responsibility is ours...not theirs. People can call, whisper, frown and talk all they want, the bottom line is that I LOVE YOU! And I want to make you happy any and everyway I can!! So put

that in your back pocket sister! ☺ *(End of discussion)*

I was a little troubled by all this, more so for my parents then for myself. This was so out-of-the-blue for them. I didn't want them to take on this unneeded worry. Were Joe's parents that upset? Why would their friend go to the trouble of looking up my parents? Did they actually think this could change my mind about Joe? This was all going through my head whenever I had a moment to think about it. When Joe's letter reached me, he validated what I was thinking and the last statement he made, "end of discussion," helped me to stop worrying about this. I had better things to do!

A new companion replaced the young girl. Soeur Wood was funny and enthusiastic and I was a little grateful she was American. I love speaking French but it was nice to relax and speak my language occasionally. Soeur Wood could play the piano amazingly well. She could take requests and play any song I could think of, even if she had never played it! My favorite song she played was "The Flight of the Bumble Bee." She would act like her hands were taking over and playing without her consent. She also made me laugh when we were riding bikes. She imitated Pee Wee Herman, humming just like him as she did her bike tricks.

We were homebound many days because she had a parasite, a little friend she brought with her from Perpignan. She named the little guy Jumi (it was part of the long name of the type of parasite she had.) She laughed even when she was in pain.

While she rested, I read the New Testament in French and remember being so impressed with how radical Jesus was. He really put people in their place. My favorite example was the instance when the woman caught committing adultery was brought to Him. Her accusers were ready to catch Jesus as they asked what should be done to her. He was so wise in His response. They didn't get either response they were looking for, "Let him who has no sin cast the first stone." What an amazing lesson for them then and for us now. Brilliant in French as well as English!

Letter from Joe:

This is something I heard in Church today that you can apply to 'The Situation' or anything else:

While praying-

We ask for strength, we get afflictions,
We ask for courage, we get dangers,
We ask for wisdom, we get problems.

We ask for favors, we get opportunities.
He gives them to us for our benefit
As He sees fit, not necessarily as we see
fit.

Traveling around isn't all that bad;
Think about it! ☺"

Statements like this always raised my anxiety. Traveling around as a military wife wasn't a concern of mine. My concerns were more about me knowing if he was *the one*. I wished I was more certain about my future with Joe. I loved him. I was continually impressed with his growing understanding of the gospel and his passion for living it. Sometimes I would think about how I would feel if he met someone else. Would I feel happy for him? Yes, but I would be jealous of the other girl. I just didn't know when we were going to have time to spend with each other in order to make any decision. But there was no sense praying about it while on my mission. I knew it wasn't the time to try and get an answer.

I had served in Yverdon-les-bains for six months when I was transferred to Geneva and was with another French companion for a month. Soeur Diosdado and I didn't always agree on our plans for the day. I was the senior companion, and I was having a hard time being in charge because she was a take-charge type person. I learned from her to not judge. One night we talked about our lives and I found out why she was so strong willed. She was forced to survive on her own from the time she was a young teenager. As I was learning more about my companion, I also received this letter from Joe. I had written him early on about having a hard time and he responded with some great advice:

Dear Darla,   *Nov. 1988*

I just received your letter after mailing mine to you. (The one you got yesterday) Anyway since I have a few minutes I want to tell you a few things about leadership and how you can do a few things to set things straight between you and your comp. The fact that you are Senior does not mean <u>anything!</u> Yes, you read what I said! It means absolutely nothing - unless you make it work for <u>you!!</u> Darla! She may not acknowledge you as Senior, because she has some ideas of her own. Nevertheless she is wrong for being difficult and not acknowledging your Seniority. I know you want to be loving and kind and not make waves, but there are times you must put your foot down for the sake of doing the Lord's work <u>correctly</u>. You shouldn't ever have to <u>tell</u> anyone you are Senior, they should be able to gather it and see it in the way you act, talk, and interact with others. <u>You</u> must <u>demand</u> <u>respect</u> from your subordinates (people under you.) I know this sounds like you have to be hard-nosed but you don't. I promise you that the leaders of the church deal with people who challenge their leadership all the time. But they are able to demand respect in a loving way that is exemplary of the way the Savior would. If you are in charge, then take hold of the situation no matter what it is. If it means that you plan the weeks ahead, then you stick to what you planned and how you think it should be done. (With the Lord's confirmation of course) If you want some of her input -then ask for it. If not then that's ok too. You, the leader, have the option to change or not, based on her input. Leadership is motivating others to accomplish an objective. Unless you find someway to motivate her then you're gonna feel angry inside no matter how you try not to let it affect you! Like you said, "Proactive not Reactive." I know it is hard to do *although I make it sound easy. It isn't easy for me either, but I've learned how to do it, so that I can get the job done and not step on too many "feelings." Darla, "Leadership" is the only thing holding back the Church in many parts of the world. The Gen. Authorities have had to slow down missionary work in some countries because there weren't enough local leaders or people with the ability to lead the Church in that area just yet. Places where hundreds of people get baptized each month and there aren't enough leaders developed enough to guide these people. Consequently people go inactive right after baptism & missionaries spend their time reactivating instead of looking for new sheep to bring into the fold. So you think about it and then take action. The Church needs good leaders, Darla; you never know what you're gonna be called to do when you return. In Germany I was one of 6 Elders in that branch that covered a big area. If I end up there after graduation then there is no telling what I may be called to. I know of 23 year old guys getting called to the <u>Stake High Council!</u> So go for what you know*

Darls, it is entirely up to D.J.C. (my initials)

Joe wasn't like my girlfriends who probably would have responded with sympathy for me in this difficult situation, instead he took it upon himself to educate me. He forced me to look at myself instead of blaming my companion. I wasn't a victim? It was my issue not hers? It wasn't a quick improvement, but I started planning ahead and was less offended by her desire to take charge.

This letter proved to be valuable years later when, once again, I felt like I was having my authority challenged. My mother-in-law is a strong, successful woman. She did a great job raising her children and she wanted so badly to help me raise mine, especially with Joe not being there to help. I wasn't very good at handling our difference of opinion and I was offended by her way too often. She was anxious to do things with the children and she would make plans with them. She would then inform me of what her plans were. I wanted to be asked. So there I was, feeling sorry for myself and praying for strength and answers, not even thinking that it was something I needed to do differently. Again I had labeled myself the victim. I then reached into my bedside drawer, which was always full of reassurance from my husband that I was loved and admired. Randomly pulling out this letter, I was instructed and inspired by my husband for the second time. Again I was forced to look at what I needed to change instead of trying to change someone else. I am slowly learning that I am only a victim when I choose to let myself be one.

He gave me a little more advice in the next letter, as well as a reminder of his love for his mother. I also appreciated the message of being loved and admired as well, which is what I was always fishing for when I opened that drawer.

...Being [LDS Institute] President is seriously going to make me improve my organizational skills. Anything involved with the Church should be done the best it can be, which means good organization, 'Proper Prior Planning Prevents P___ Poor Performance.' Army saying! Anyway, I'm glad I've got the job.

...You know, I brag about you constantly. "I have the best missionary in the world!!" Just a few minutes ago I

was telling Mark how you used to make me open the door for you whenever we got out of a car. 'That' I told him "is a true lady." I never told you but I appreciated that greatly! Thank you, I love you.

...I'm sure you are aware that today was Mother's Day. I talked to my Mommy today and told her I love her. Gosh if they only knew how much! I wanted to at least mail your mother a card and tell her thanks for being the mother of the most beautiful, intelligent, sincere, loving, caring, hard working, humble, athletic, genuine girl in the world! (I think that covers everything) But I was afraid they would not know what to think of me, so I took a chill pill. ☺

My last companion was another French girl. She was actually part Moroccan and part Russian, but had lived in the south of France most of her life. I had a hard time calling her the appropriate "Sister so and so" because I loved her first name, Feiza. She was "Feiza" to me when we weren't at church or teaching on the streets. She cracked me up and taught me some essential French phrases, such as, ten different ways to tell someone to get away from you. She sang hymns as we walked down the street and she talked incessantly! I miss her still. It was amusing to talk to people in the streets with her. In Geneva there are so many languages spoken. We never knew if we were approaching someone who spoke French or German or Spanish or Italian...but with Feiza we covered most of them. She spoke Arabic, Spanish, and Portuguese, besides French—and her English wasn't too bad either.

When we were alone, we would mix French, English and some Spanish. So when I returned to the states I would unknowingly throw words in here and there which made no sense to English-only speaking people. I also had a hard time remembering some English words. I would say something and then have to ask if I just used an understandable word. I used to get annoyed with returned missionaries who would struggle with English words. I thought they were showing off: "My mission really helped my.....what is that word... oh yeah... faith...in the Lord..." I would think, "Yeah right you want us to believe you just forgot your own language!?" So now I was the one annoying those ignorant-of-the-experience listeners who would judge me the way I had judged others. Just like the scripture! ("Judge not, that ye be not judged. Or with what judgment ye judge, ye shall be judged..." Matthew 7:1)

One time as my companion and I ran to the mail box and eagerly thumbed through the mail, I started smiling because I recognized that beautiful handwriting.

Feiza quickly snatched it from my grasp and said in her cute French accent; "It is for me, it is for me!"

I looked at it again and was shocked to see her name on it! She quickly opened it and began to read. It was a letter of encouragement from Joe. I had shared with him in the previous letter that her parents didn't want her to be on a mission, they didn't want her to be Mormon, and she wasn't getting very much mail. He could relate to her better than I could. She was not only inspired by his words but grateful to know that she wasn't the only one dealing with this issue. This is a lesson I would later learn—how precious it is, when dealing with something difficult, to find another to relate to. Joe had already learned this lesson. Now I ask, are there many guys out there who would have done that? I didn't think so. It made me love him even more.

It's me again. I just wanted to tell you about some other things. Yesterday we, W.P. Branch, played the Newburgh Ward in B-ball. Yes we won, not by enough though. And yes I gave a clinic, but I didn't charge admission this time!

☺

Today me and some of the guys who stopped playing B-ball for West Point are getting together and having a scrimmage game against the junior Varsity team. It's funny because all of us should be playing Varsity right now, but for different reasons we all quit to pursue other interests, mainly academics.

It was too bad that Joe had to stop playing basketball in order to keep up with the West Point curriculum because he really could "put on a clinic!" He loved to play and I loved hearing about him playing and being reminded of how it all started. (With a dunk!)

The time for me to go home drew near and I was very nervous about what I was going to do next. Worrying about my own life was not nearly as fun as worrying about others. The other missionaries knew of my anxiety so when we got together for our weekly meeting to talk about goals and progress, they would request to sing hymns like: "The time is far spent, there is little remaining…" and "God be with you till we meet again…" They were serving the Lord but they were still young men who found joy in teasing. My stomach would jump as I was hit with my many worries. *Where am I going to live? Where am I going to finish my bachelor's degree? What's going to happen with Joe and me?* I was also uneasy about ending my mission because I wasn't sure I had done everything I was sent there to do.

Dearestest Darlita,   *7 Feb 1989*

Hi! How are you? ...you need to find a seat because I've got more good news than you will be able to handle. For starters, with the info I've already provided you about my Basic Course and Ranger School, I have recently discovered that I have a more than good chance of remaining here in the states for my first assignment. (This means not Germany!!) In the practice poll I got Fort Riley, Kansas. We've just been notified that there are more slots available to us for Riley so I'll probably get that on Feb. 15. Fort Riley is about 17 miles from Kansas State Univ., so there will be plenty to do. Also it is a 1 ½ day drive from Arizona.

Okay, so that was the good news!! Yaaaay!! Now for the absolutely incredible news!! Yesterday I was approached by one of the basketball coaches and asked if I wanted to be a GRADUATE ASSISTANT COACH! Yes, it's all true! What does this mean? Well I'll tell you. This means that I'll be an assistant coach either here or the West Point Preparatory School in N.J. (which is where I would rather go.)

This also means that I won't go to my Officer Basic Course until next spring and Ranger School in the summer of 1990. Further more I'll have this whole summer off (I think.) I'll also get paid extra $! But probably the most important aspect of this is that I will be able to pick my own assignment which could be in California, Hawaii, Italy, and a number of places!

Now what does this do for you and I? It gives us the most precious commodity you and I need...<u>time</u>! With all of that extra time we can make our decisions and have the opportunity to do things right, so we are not rushed too much. This Darla, is my driving force behind accepting this job, besides loving basketball. ☺

I still have to talk to the Athletic Director here at W.P. and then get approved militarily by the commandant, Gen. Gordon. But the paper work is in the process and I'm gearing up for it. I wish I could've asked you how you felt about all this and get a response before it all happened but that is impossible. However I did seek Heavenly Father's guidance and I feel good about it, so we'll see how it turns out. It's been funny to think that I'm possibly making decisions for two and not just me. Well, Darla I hope that you haven't been totally flabbergasted by all this but I know you're interested! There hasn't been too much else happening around here lately that I haven't already told you. I tried to call Dennis & Carolyn but they've either moved or their phone is disconnected. I wish I knew when Dale was going through JFK so I could meet him, but I can't get in touch. I would call your folks but I don't know how well that would go over with them. I still might do it anyway just to show 'em I'm not the big bad wolf who's gonna steal their Goldilocks away. ☺ *However, I am gonna be the Prince*

Charming that comes to sweep their Cinderella off her feet and then live happily ever after!! I don't think they'll like that one either!

I Love you dearly! Take care and keep up the good work. Remember, I'm here waiting for you! ☺

His letters were adding to my end-of-the-mission anxiety, he was planning our future together and I just didn't know how it would work. I encouraged him to take advantage of being able to coach at West Point. It sounded like a fun job. I also expressed my confidence in his ability to make decisions for himself. I just couldn't concentrate too much on what would happen after my mission because Feiza and I were so busy. With her being able to speak Spanish, we were teaching a lot of people from South America. We had a full schedule and not much time to think about anything but missionary work.

Dearestest Darla,　　　　　*23 Feb 1989*

Did you receive the tape and pictures yet? I hope so! I have one more small piece of info to add to the picture...I start my officer Basic Course on 8 Jan

1990, so I'll probably report on the 6th. Now I just want to take the time to tell you just how special a person you are in my life! ☺ I got 3 letters this week from the young lady whom I most adore. You! I'm so glad that you are pleased with my decisions. I was worried because some officers told me I may start off behind the power curve by not going straight to my first assignment. But I know there was a reason for me to get this opportunity at this particular time, so I took it in hand. Ya know, last night it took me a while to fall asleep after I said my prayers because I was thinking of just how much I really do love you. I can remember just looking at you and watching you walk! ☺ I used to watch all your mannerisms, because I just couldn't believe a girl could be everything I could imagine. Today in a welding lab we were going over a problem (that I still can't do) and my mind was off somewhere remembering how you feel in my arms and how you are the perfect height for me so I don't break my neck kissing you.

I also thought about how incredibly different you were than me; how the knowledge you had transcended my wildest imagination. Even after I was baptized and we partook of the sacrament together, I was still only in the door. But now I have learned so much more and I marvel at how close two people can be especially when they share the same understanding and love each other dearly. I can't even imagine what it will be like to sit down and study & discuss the word of God with the woman I love.

I can't wait to walk around the "magic Kingdom" hand in hand with you, knowing that we share a common knowledge about the purpose of life. I know that sounds weird but I'll remind you of it and you will feel what I'm talking about. Sometimes it's hard to imagine us anywhere except W.P. and New Rochelle. I'm looking forward to making new lasting memories.

Do you have any idea of what it is going to be like sitting in the celestial room together? [In the Temple] I cannot think of a more dramatic or even traumatic turn of events since 21 Feb. 1987. I remember how taken away I was the first time I did baptisms for the dead, and how remarkable it was to be in the House of the Lord. I remember sitting there and wondering "What am I doing here?" And "How has this all come about?" Now I know...my P. [patriarchal] blessing says...

'While you lived in his presence in the pre-existent world you made <u>decisions</u> and <u>choices</u> which bring you here into mortality at this time, that placed you in the <u>circumstances</u> that you were <u>raised</u> in and brought you into <u>"the situations"</u> which brought you into The Church of Jesus Christ of Latter-day Saints. ...'

Darla it seems as though decisions and choices are what decide the situations we place ourselves in. And now as I read that part of my P-blessing I understand why I have seemed to have made some pretty good decisions so far in my life. I guess that is why I'm so happy about our situation, although I know it won't be easy at all; but then I have yet to read in the scriptures, in my P-blessing, or hear a General Authority say anything about anything in life being easy. Anything worthwhile and lasting is not easy. I think of Abraham and how <u>hard</u> it must've been for him to sacrifice his only son so that he might be the father of nations. And it was because of his faith and making the <u>hard decision</u> and <u>choosing</u> to offer his only son that God stayed his hand, and poured on him the blessings of the Fatherhood of all nations.

I look forward to the opportunity we will have in just a few months to sit down and make decisions and choices together, and I don't care if we're just choosing what restaurant to eat at I just want to do it with you.

Darla I hope you have a feel for how much I care about you. And look forward to the time when I can walk around here with you holding on to my "iron rod" (arm) because I know with it I can make you happy. ☺

I hope you realize how very much I Love You and admire you for all that you do for me. There is nobody else I would rather have stand tall next to me than you providing a pillar of support when we confront our parents, friends *and neighbors. You have no idea of how much I'm looking forward to that time. They will only be obstacles if we take our eyes off the goal and "look beyond the mark."*

Choices and Decisions Darla, from now on they are for keeps and there will be no turning back!

I Love you Darla!

Always & Forever,

Joe

PS. In the next few weeks you should be getting an invitation from the Daughters of the US Army to attend a function for those young ladies who are getting married to a cadet within the next year. Although we're not engaged I thought I'd see if you could go to find out about the Army from an Officer's wife's point of view! K?

Whew, his letter had me freaking out! Excited, nervous, anxious; I was a mess!

As my day of departure was approaching, April 14, 1989, I made sure that Joe had my flight plans. I was flying through New York and Joe planned to be there to see me. This made me very nervous because I looked so different and I was worried he would take one look at my croissant and chocolate-eatin' face and say, "This is what I've been so anxiously waiting for?" A few days before I was to leave, the mission president called me and told me that they had rescheduled our flight plans for four days later because of the threat of a terrorist attack on that day. In my little sheltered life I had never heard about terrorists and their threats, it was something I didn't truly understand. I talked to the mission secretary and made sure he could call my family and Joe to let them know of the change.

The delay turned out to be quite a treat for me. I was able to go to the little village of Fribourg, Switzerland. The first time I went to Fribourg was when I was serving in Yverdon, just a short beautiful train ride away. I loved this village from the first moment I stepped off the train. I felt like I was in a fairytale. Most villages in Switzerland have that look, but in Fribourg, I wouldn't have been surprised if the seven dwarfs came whistling up the cobble stone street!

I had the privilege of working with my first companion (in the MTC) who I loved and admired.

She was not only motivating, she was hysterical! She introduced the word "bionic" to me. I was bionic, she was bionic, we were bionic together; we were so bionic we were doing "split-leaps!" (Another word I picked up from her) She had me doing split-leaps throughout my mission! So Cardon and I, the bionic team, did split-leaps in Fribourg. We actually were able to participate in a baptism which took place in a public indoor swimming pool.

With the change of flight plans we were no longer flying through New York, but through Chicago. I was kind of relieved because I was seriously stressing over seeing Joe, or more so of him seeing me. When I arrived in Arizona, the scene I had dreamt about my whole mission felt like I was still in a dream. After eighteen months of being away I was back in my family's arms. They were all there except Dale, who had left on his mission to England just a few months prior.

My family later confirmed my fear of scaring Joe with my new look. My oldest brother, David, said I looked like I was wearing a nun dress, and they all made comments about my tight poodle perm. To make me look even worse, because I was struggling to keep my eyes open, I had them open so wide I looked bug-eyed. I won't mind if the video of that event is eternally lost. I not only felt like I was in the twilight zone I looked like it too!

I found out later, the mission secretary did not get a message to Joe and he was waiting in the airport with roses in hand on April 14th. It still disturbs me to think about this moment of disappointment and frustration for him.

CHAPTER 7

Through the Fire

When I got home, I called Joe. He had already made plans for me to fly to New York to be there for his graduation, along with a month's worth of traveling. From New York we would drive down the East Coast to the DC Temple and then to his home in Orlando and then we would fly to my home in Arizona. I wasn't sure about us and he could tell I was uneasy as we spoke for the first time. I hadn't shared these travel plans with my parents yet and I wasn't sure how they were going to react. "Mom, Dad, I love Joe, and I am going to spend a month with him in a few weeks." I only remember bits and pieces of that conversation. "So and so (blonde-hair-blue-eyes) has been asking about you. Why would you want to make your life harder? Your children won't be accepted by either race. Marriage is hard even when you are the same race." They reminded me of the phone call they had received early one morning from a "concerned friend" who didn't like that we were dating each other. "Why would you want to bring this kind of drama into your life?" They weren't happy with me, but I let them know that I would not change my plans. I didn't like going against my parents wishes but I had to find out how I really felt about Joe and to do that, I had to spend time with him.

My journal entry:

May 15, 1989

Well, I'm on the plane again, off to NY this time. I've been day dreaming about this day for so long, it's hard to believe it's finally here. I'm excited but extremely nervous! I was at home yesterday and talked with everyone. Dawney, Gene, Tim and Danette all gave me their advice and ideas on what would be in my future if I was to be married to Joe. It's really all about our children and the problems they would have from others who are prejudiced and how much it will hurt us to see our children suffer. Even if they do understand life - Heavenly Fathers plan and His gospel, that still won't make up for kids calling names and not feeling accepted because they're different. Right now I'm just really tired of stressing over it! I felt awful last night when Mom asked me how long I would be staying. I could see her heart drop when I said "three weeks." They are so worried about me, I hate putting them through this but I can't just drop everything to please them. I have to make this decision myself and I really wish they would trust and stand behind me in the decision I make. Right now my stomach hurts because I'm stressing so much, my heart and my mind are both having major work outs. I'm so confused! But I know what to do. The Lord will help and guide me through this. I know Joe and I will both make the right choice. Right now what I need is one big chill pill! In other words: prayer and scriptures! ☺ (The Sunday school answers!)

Joe looked more handsome than I remembered. As I approached him he handed me a rose and said, "welcome home." His smile calmed the butterflies in my stomach. We then walked side by side to baggage claim. For a year and a half I did not date. It was against mission rules to be alone with a guy, so as much as I had grown to love Joe, it felt very awkward to be with him. It didn't help that my wardrobe was out-dated and didn't fit, and I didn't know what to do with my frizzed-out hair. Love really is blind. It was with Joe anyway. He later said he had faith that the real me would come back. It didn't take long for me to feel comfortable with him as he directed me through the airport and to his car. He opened the passenger door to his black Beretta to let me in and then grabbed a book out of the seat and handed it to me before he closed the door. Once he got in his car, he explained that he had been working on this photo album throughout my mission. It was full of pictures of both of us, with little witty subtitles he had cut out of magazines and newspapers. As I turned the last page, on the left side it read, **"Our story continues… Happily Ever After?"** and on the right was a picture of the Washington Temple. It made me nervous. I knew at that point I couldn't go on much longer not being sure about my future with him.

As we talked about the possibilities of our future together, we weighed the pros and cons. Most of the cons were about *others*; our parents, what *others* would think, what *others* thought our children would have to deal with, how the prejudices of *others* would affect Joe being able to advance in his career—a worry put into our heads by *others*.

Now let's hear it for the pros! The pros were about how much we loved each other and how strong we both were. We knew we could handle the shallow-mindedness of *others*! We would teach our children of their infinite worth and about God's plan for them. We read our patriarchal blessings and read scriptures together and we prayed together. My love quadrupled for Joe in just a couple days, I trusted that he would always do what was right for both of us because his goals were based on his desire to follow God.

I stayed with Brother and Sister Guthrie. They'd let me stay with them a couple times when I was a nanny and it was great to spend time with them again. The third night I was there, we didn't stay out as late because Joe had an early meeting. I was able to get a hold of my brother, Dennis, by phone, to get his opinion. He said he had been thinking about me all day and he came to the conclusion that it wasn't for him to decide. He said that if we get inspiration from heaven that we are right for each other then we can't let everyone else's opinions stop us. Having his blessing meant a lot to me. I've always looked up to him and taken his advice. *Inspiration from heaven.* The phrase he used hit me hard. It's time! I resolved as I hung up with him to go up to my room and have a chat with God. But before I could make it upstairs this nice couple I was staying with, stopped me half way up with a request to talk. That wasn't in my plan but I'm glad I came back down to talk. They went on and on about what an amazing person Joe was and how they would love for their daughter to marry someone just like him. They had been close by as Joe was baptized and as he was called to be the vice president of the LDS Institute and then as the president his senior year. Brother Guthrie had laid his hands on Joe's head and bestowed the priesthood upon him. As much as I thought I knew Joe through his letters, they had been with him and witnessed his strength of spirit and character.

I couldn't wait to get up to my room to pray after we spoke. I hit my knees and pleaded with my Heavenly Father to tell me if Joe was the one. I thought of everything my parents had said, everything his friends who I was staying with had said, his letters, the change he had made, how I felt about him, how he felt about me. I loved him, but for me it wasn't a matter of, "Would I like to marry him." It was the question of, "Was it meant to be?" Or to put it better, "Was it God's will that Joe and I be together?" I was on my knees for quite some time when I finally asked, "Am I supposed to marry Joe?" As I said the words I received that familiar strong feeling of happiness and certainty, a feeling I could not question. I knew I was supposed to marry him! I knew that it was God's will. It took a long time for me to fall asleep. I lay in bed with a big smile on my face, "I am going to marry Joe!" The next morning I awoke to my new reality, "I'm going to marry Joe?" I slide out of bed onto my knees to ask again. "I know I had that great feeling and my prayer was answered but could I have that again? Am I supposed to marry Joe?" I again received a feeling I could not question, "I *am* going to marry Joe!" I knew, I finally knew! I couldn't wait to tell him!

The time to tell him didn't come fast enough. After his meeting, we worked out. We got cleaned up. We ate breakfast in a busy restaurant. We watched the cadet parade and he introduced me to professors and friends. At last we were alone as we drove to New Rochelle to visit with the Coopers. I told him I had something important to tell him and then I replayed the events of the night and that morning. As I announced that I knew we were supposed to be married, he said, "Hmm" and then he turned the radio on. *What? All this time he has thrown out little hints of proposing and letting me know that he was sure and I haven't been sure and now I say that I'm sure and all he has to say is, "Hmm!?"* I turned the radio off, "Did you get what I just said?"

"I just need to think about what you just said." Again the radio went on and we didn't say another word for the rest of the trip.

I was relieved when we pulled up in front of that familiar house on Disbrow Lane. The silence between us was torture. I love the Coopers. Doug was still full of jokes and Terry was just as sweet, Josh and Abs weren't so little anymore but still as cute. I felt as comfortable as if I were with family even though we hadn't seen each other or communicated in almost two years. I really enjoyed our visit. I have them to thank for letting me work for them and encouraging me to go to West Point.

On our way back, the radio stayed on for a while and then Joe turned it off and said, "Now tell me that story again. What happened last night and this morning?" I repeated the details of my prayer and how it was answered. He shared with me that he had always known but he hadn't thought to pray about it. Before we got to West Point, Joe stopped at a park called Bear Mountain. We walked where there were a lot of picnic tables, the same tables we had eaten at on those first few dates two years previous. He sat me down at one of them, got on one knee and smiled at me… I like the way he tells it…

Joe's journal:

Then I sat her down on a bench, descended to one knee and uttered these memorable words, "Darla, will you marry me?" With a glow in eyes, a smile and a playful hesitation she said "yes!" My day had been made one million

> *times over. I always dreamed of that moment when I would propose to the woman I love. I only wish I could've had a ring to give her.*

For a moment we were both in heaven, we were ready to commit to each other, to spend forever with each other, and nothing else mattered!

That blissful feeling changed the next day as I met his parents. They were cordial to me but I could tell they were anything but thrilled to be in my presence. His mother could hardly bare to look at me.

Joe described it well in a journal entry:

> *From that night on things went down hill at zero slope.*

I never thought an engagement was supposed to be filled with so much opposition. It's good I had had an answer twice because I had to refer to that experience many times. I'd say to myself, "I did get that answer; we are supposed to get married. This is God's will!" The strong answer that I'd received kept me moving forward, as we were jumping over hurdle after hurdle.

We didn't tell anyone of our plans to marry right away. There were less than a handful of people who were happy for us to be together. To say that our parents were unhappy about us is an understatement. We knew that announcing our engagement would have sent them over the edge. At one point I called home and talked to my mother. She was very tense. She wanted me to come home. I let her know when I would be flying back to Arizona from Florida and that Joe would be coming with me. As soon as I said that, I heard a "click."

Joe was right by my side at the pay phone booth. I turned and blurted out in disbelief, "She hung up on me!" I was in shock. My mother and I had never been in an argument like that.

I was shocked even more when Joe started laughing and said "GOOD! Now you get a little taste of what I've been dealing with!" I didn't get a bit of sympathy from him!

It wasn't supposed to be like this. I had watched movies where there was a big dinner party at a fancy restaurant and everyone was smiling and then the happy couple announced their plans to marry, which brought on instant applause and cheers and congratulations. We would never have such a party. Ours was a scene of anger and sadness. I wrote my parents a long letter describing Joe's character and how much I loved him and that I had prayed about

Joe from day one.

The rain poured down during his graduation. My umbrella only kept the rain out of my face, but didn't keep me from getting absolutely soaked. I sat by myself thinking about the past: meeting him, my mission, my parents, his parents. It seemed overwhelming to think of everyone who would oppose our marriage. The rain seemed to be symbolic of the storms ahead of us. After the graduation I stood awkwardly by as his family hugged, congratulated him, and took pictures. I felt like an intruder. They clearly did not want me to be a part of their moment with their son.

They had planned a graduation party for him that weekend in New Jersey and they made it clear to Joe that I was not invited. Joe had me stay with his old basketball coach from prep school. This family and I had a small moment to get to know each other before Joe left. They didn't understand, "Why wasn't I going to his graduation party?" they wanted to know. All I have to say is: awkward!

Late that night when Joe returned, he was very anxious and questioning everything, "I don't know if we'll be able to go through with this, my parents will make it impossible!" I assumed his whole family had had quite a chat with him. This is where that answer to my prayer was the only thing I could hold on to. I had to be the strong one. I reminded him of all the time he had wanted us to be together and planned on our marrying and how my prayer was answered, and that if God wanted us to get married, then we would get married.

The rest of our trip was like a roller coaster as we enjoyed each other's company and then stressed over the opposition ahead of us as we tried to plan a life together. In Orlando I stayed with a family Joe had met while attending church during school breaks. They had invited him to dinner the first time they saw him at church. What a breath of fresh air they were! J'Deene and George Parkhurst were so happy to meet me! They stayed up late talking to me about how they met Joe, how much they loved him, how they heard all about me and how happy they would be to see us married. Oh, how I needed them in my life right then!

Every morning J'Deene would give me a huge bear hug, a hug that would release all the stress I was feeling. She would tell me how happy she was to have me in her home and how much love she felt for both Joe and me. There will always be a special place in my heart for this wonderful family who helped strengthen and lift me when it seemed the world was against us.

I did visit Joe's home and I got to meet Joe's sisters, Vonda and Daria, and his cousin, Samantha, who was living with them. They were really nice to me. Daria asked how we met and made me laugh as she told me stories of her boyfriends. His mother and

I had a private talk about Joe and me. She suggested I come to live in Orlando and work and finish school while Joe could get himself established. She let me know that it would not be wise to get married too soon, without their blessing. They wanted us to wait but I figured their hope was that Joe would come to his senses and not marry me at all. I listened but I didn't agree. Joe shared with me one of their views: I didn't have a degree or a career, "What was I bringing to the party?"

As we flew to Arizona together we knew we would be greeted by Danette but I still hadn't communicated with my parents since that heated phone conversation with my mother. I didn't know if Joe would be meeting my parents or not. Danette and her husband, Tim, lived in Tucson at the time. When we got to Danette's home, she announced that Mom wanted me to call her. My eyebrows rose, not knowing if this was good or bad news. My stomach was in knots as I dialed that familiar number. My mother answered and I hesitated to talk, but I forced myself to say, "Hi" and to let her know that we were at Danette's.

She shocked me with a cheerful greeting, and she continued to surprise me with her plans to have us come that weekend.

"Would Joe rather have steak or chicken?"

My letter must have helped, I thought.

We experienced our own, "Guess Who's Coming to Dinner!" As we drove up to my home, the home I had lived in from birth to high school graduation, I felt nervous! My little brother and sister stood behind the screen door just staring at us, which made me more nervous, but it made Joe laugh. Joe had joked about messing with my family and greeting them with some street talk: "Yo yo, what's up Pops? Nice crib!"

My brother and sister continued to stare at Joe, which he laughed about later. As we were in the front room with the TV on, they turned to look at him every time someone black came on the screen. In the small city of Willcox, (Home of the Fighting Cowboys) there were only a few black families. I don't think the family had ever had them over for dinner, so this was a new experience for them. I was so grateful to my parents for making Joe feel welcome and conversation flowed quite well. It didn't take long for them to like him.

Joe got so comfortable that when Mom had asked him a question; a "Do you want this or that" type question, he responded with, "It don't make me no neva' mind." I gave him such a look. I had never heard him say that before! I didn't know if that was something he said regularly or if he just brought that one out to mess with me.

My parents later explained their change of heart. That particular month the church magazine, the Ensign, was filled with the talks that had been given the previous month in general conference. The talk that the prophet, President Benson, had given was on pride. My parents were humble enough to take a hard look at themselves as they read that address, and realized they needed to change their way of thinking about race. They also had some good friends who helped them look at the good qualities Joe had. They now liked him, but they were still uneasy about us being married. In their minds this was going to make our lives so difficult. The reality was that the only difficult part of our relationship was convincing our parents that we could be happy together!

I was so grateful to be talking to Mom again, and grateful that both my parents were willing to consider our ideas. I somehow thought that things would also get easier with Joe's parents but that wasn't the case. They were being forced to deal with too many changes in Joe. They were also being forced to deal with the fact that they wouldn't be able to go into the temple to see their son get married. Only those who have gone through the temple (worthy members of the Church) could be inside.

It didn't work like the movies I've watched where everything seemed to get resolved in one day, or one weekend. Opinions and perceptions aren't changed so easily and instantly.

Joe's journal:

Aug 1989

> *I can't believe this is really happening to my family because we are so close. I can't help but remember times of harmony and love in our home, when it seemed that nothing could tear us apart. I love them so much that I often wonder is this really all worth putting them through. I just can't help but think that I would be 1,000 times more sorry if I were to forsake my love for Darla and my covenants with the Lord.*

This was not what they had planned for their son's future. They thought he was digging a hole for himself. He was starting out his adult life with three strikes against him: First, he's black; second, he's Mormon; and third, he has a white wife! For them, this spelled out a difficult life with no chance for advances because of the prejudices of others. They did everything in their power to stop Joe from making such a mess of his life. He dealt with more tears and pleadings and hurtful words than his heart could stand.

I didn't fully comprehend the fear that both of our parents shared as they imagined our future together. Joe's parents had lived through the civil rights era. They had experienced bigotry close up and in person and couldn't imagine their son not having the same experiences. My mom lived in an area where the black children went to a different school, and the black families in the small town were in a separate neighborhood. This really wasn't an issue in our small town because there weren't enough black families. So my parents never experienced any civil rights changes. They were still remembering their experience with segregation and couldn't imagine their grandchildren fitting in. They were worried for my safety as well as their grandchildren's well being. Joe's mom called mine at one point and expressed her fear for her son's safety. Both our mothers had lived through a time when a black man could be killed for being seen with a white woman. I was oblivious to these issues but I was trying to educate myself by reading black history. But that's what it still was for me – history – not something I needed to worry about now or in our future.

I went to the temple early one Saturday morning. I had arrived so early that it was not yet open so I decided to walk around the grounds. It was a beautiful morning and I was ready to take in the scenery: the flowers, the trees, the pools of water reflecting the white building. As I turned the corner I was surprised to see a crowd of people, and in the middle of that crowd was a bride and groom getting their picture taken. I could see both sets of parents there, everyone was smiling, everyone was happy. I stared silently as tears flowed down my cheeks. *Would there be anyone smiling at our wedding? Why Father, why? Why does it have to be so hard for us?*

Joe stayed at West Point after graduation to be a grad assistant coach for the basketball team. I got a job at Naturally Women as a weight trainer in Tucson. I lived with my sister Danette, and her family. We made plans to get married in August 1990, right after he finished Infantry Officer Basic Course (IOBC) at Ft. Benning, Georgia. My parents slowly accepted the fact that Joe and I were going to get married, though that didn't mean they were happy about it.

One night Joe's sisters called me. One of them told me how sad her family had become since I came into the picture. The other told me to please break it off with their brother for awhile. As I hung up I slid down the wall and sobbed. Being told that I was making everyone in their family sad overwhelmed me. I've always gone out of my way to make others happy and to avoid contention. I didn't like upsetting anyone. Now I was being told that I had single handedly torn a family apart and caused extreme sadness to come into their home. I had a lot of time alone to think about what we could do and I came up with the perfect solution. We could fake a break up for them. This was my "try to please everyone" way of thinking.

When Joe called later that night, I was almost hysterical as I told him about the phone call, "We have to pretend that we break up, and then we can get back together, they are so sad, they said it's all my fault, they said…"

"No!" Joe interrupted me. "Listen to me and stop this craziness! We will not play any game like that. We will be honest with my family. We're getting married and you are not the reason for their sadness!"

I instantly felt ashamed of myself for planning this lie for his family. I had gotten myself so worked up that I wasn't thinking straight. Joe was a rock, he was my hero. I was reminded of why I love him so much. He had integrity even when it was hard. He didn't look for the easy way out if it wasn't the honest way.

I felt bad for Joe, but I didn't truly understand what he was going through with his parents, and I couldn't comprehend the profound sacrifice he was making. He was a high achiever and had always pleased his parents—until now.

We debated about the wedding date. We moved it forward from August 1990 to January 1990 a few times and then back. One night, I'm sure after a heated conversation with his parents, he called me and firmly stated that we were getting married in January and that was that—no more changes! He told me that he didn't want to wait. He didn't think he could take the pressure his parents were putting on him for much longer. He said he was tired of waiting, hurting, and worrying about the marriage, his parents, and how they'd take it. He spoke of eloping to the newly dedicated Oregon Temple—no reception, no dinners, away from any family or friends. As he spoke, I was speechless. *But my parents have accepted us. They want to be there*, I thought. I felt my heart break as I thought of my wedding day without my family. Instantly, I thought of how selfish I'd been to expect Joe to be grateful for the fact that at least my family was ready to support us and be there when his family would not. How could he be happy about his wedding day without his family there by his side as he had always imagined. I told him to let me think about it.

After I hung up, I started sobbing as I prayed to know what to do. I poured out my heart to God, *What's going to happen? Why does it have to be so hard for us to be together? What should we do? Should we elope? Is this what's best for Joe?* I felt so alone and unsure of all the decisions I'd made. As I started to cry again, the strangest feeling came over me and I felt the pressure of a hand on my shoulder. Although I was a little frightened at first, a comforting feeling came over me. The feeling of the hand on my shoulder stayed for a moment. It brought peace into my troubled heart with the realization that my decisions had been correct and that Heavenly Father would help me get through the difficult times. I felt calm and at peace. "It's going to be all right," came into my mind and filled my soul. When I couldn't feel the pressure of the hand anymore, I turned to see if I saw anyone, but all I saw was a dark empty room. I sat there for awhile, in awe of what had just happened and thanking the Lord in prayer for this blessing of comfort. I continue to wonder who that heavenly messenger was, maybe one of my grandparents or maybe it was one of Joe's distant ancestors. Who ever it was—they confirmed again for me that Joe and I were meant to be together. I resolved to be supportive of whatever Joe wanted to do. I called him the next day and recounted my experience and assured him that I would be okay with his plans for January.

By the next week, Joe had decided that we should still get married in January, but it should be in Arizona where my family could attend. My parents seemed fine with the change of dates but they didn't like the idea of us starting our lives together in Georgia. My mom envisioned skin heads and burning crosses. I assured her that we would be careful, and I was pretty sure that Georgia had progressed past that sort of thing.

Joe let his parents know about the date being moved up. They were devastated and worked even harder to change his mind.

In August Joe surprised me again. He was very serious when he stated, over the phone, that we needed to get married much sooner, next week, or next month! He said that his parents had paid a visit to Salt Lake City and they didn't have a good experience. He wanted the pleadings and pain to stop. He wanted to get it over with and be married! I told him I would marry him whenever and wherever he wanted, but as I said that, inside, I was freaking out! When will this madness stop?

Joe came to visit that same week and we set the date for October 7th. I didn't tell my mom because we were still unsure about this and she was already making plans for a reception. I think it helped Joe to have an earlier date to look to. Joe gave a talk in my ward (congregation) in Tucson Sunday afternoon and then we traveled to Willcox where he spoke at a fireside. Many people from the community as well as our church attended as he also talked about life as a West Point cadet. As I was able to hear him speak both times—about his life, his convictions, and his strong determination to follow Christ, I knew that I could do whatever it took to marry him. I couldn't imagine living my life without him. I loved him so much.

Days later, Joe rethought his idea. He had written down the pros and cons of eloping and the cons won. We impatiently waited for January to arrive. The spiritual experience I had had helped me to stay hopeful as we trudged forward toward our wedding day.

From the time I turned 12, I had been taught the importance of the law of chastity, God's law to keep a sexual relationship inside the bounds of marriage. I heard it over and over again as I attended different church meetings. I think it was a blessing to have been a skinny little underdeveloped teenager because I had time to decide for myself that when a boy did ask me out, I would have rules. This resolve helped as I started dating, I wanted to save myself for my wedding night and no boy could change my mind. When Joe and I were first dating, he let me know that he was impressed with my standards because the idea of waiting for marriage appealed to him as well. As we both had that resolve and we had made covenants with God in His temple to stay chaste, it was good that we were not physically together too much during our engagement. It wasn't easy, but we were both determined and we looked forward to the time when we could "throw away the rule book!"

I was able to visit him in October and we actually had some stress-free fun that week. Besides going to the DC Temple together, we went dancing, out to dinner, to a West Point football game, and to the city (New York City.) Having this time together really helped to keep us going for another two months wait!

We counted how many days we had actually been together, from the time we met, February 21, 1987 to our wedding day, January 2, 1990. In almost three years, we had only been physically together for a total of sixty days. It was through letters, tapes and phone calls that we had gotten to know each other. We were more honest and open about our goals and dreams for the future when we were not face to face. We were also more personal and to the point about our feelings and I think we got to know each other better that way. There is a line from the French story, "The Little Prince" that I liked to say to Joe, "J'aime celui que tu es." It means: I love who you are. That seemed to reach deeper to describe how I really felt about him. I didn't just love him. I loved his character, his integrity, his sense of humor, his spiritual strength. I loved who he was.

CHAPTER 8

For All Eternity

It seemed impossible but our wedding day finally came. Joe had a few friends and family there to support him: his roommate from West Point, Kurt Kason, as his best man; the Guthries, his friends who I had stayed with while visiting West Point; and his grandparents and Great Aunt Anna Mae from Jersey. He was grateful to have them there but his heart ached to have *all* of his family with him to share this monumental day.

We were married and sealed for eternity in the Mesa Arizona Temple. The ceremony was performed by my great uncle, Floyd Batman. His name is pronounced Batmen, but Joe liked the idea of *Batman* marrying us, so he pronounced it the "right way." A temple marriage is very different from a traditional marriage. There is no walking down an aisle or candles or flower girls in the ceremony. But it is a beautiful ceremony with a beautiful purpose. I knew it was all worth it when we looked into each others eyes as we were being sealed for time and all eternity. When we stood and looked into mirrors that are on each side of the room so that they reflect each other, we could not see an end to our reflection together. "As you stay worthy and work together, there will be no end to your union just as there is no end to your reflection." That is what it was all about. That is why Joe sacrificed so much. There was no other way we wanted to be married. Why get married for just this lifetime when we wanted to love each other and be husband and wife forever? How could we cut ourselves off like that? There was no other choice.

The rest of the day was a little crazy, a little fun, a little frustrating and a little like a fairytale (the happily ever after part). The photographer we hired to take pictures at the temple wasn't there when we made our grand exit from the main temple doors. We had to call him and wait as he made his way to us. Joe's grandparents did not understand why they weren't able to go inside to watch the wedding, and they didn't like waiting in the foyer. As we took pictures on the temple grounds, I noticed some smiles. It was better than I imagined.

After a luncheon, we all traveled to my little town

of Willcox for the reception in the cultural hall/gymnasium, which is in the center of most Mormon church buildings. It was free to use and it could be decorated. I had been to many receptions in that gym. This was what I had grown accustomed to. It was much later when it dawned on me that this was very foreign to Joe. He probably imagined a more elaborate reception, but he smiled through it all. We did have a DJ and we danced to our favorite song, "Here and Now," by Luther Vandross. I was so grateful to my co-workers from Naturally Women, who attended the reception. They brought a little more diversity to the party! They had also organized a bridal shower for me a month before. My mother had worked hard to make the reception nice. I know I didn't appreciate it enough at the time. My sister, Dawney, had car trouble and wasn't able to make it so my sister-in-law, Carolyn, became a bridesmaid. Friends from my home town and friends from college were there. I was surrounded by loved ones and I was happy.

That night, during the reception, snow started to fall heavily. One old cowboy approached Joe and said, with a strong drawl, "You're gonna have ta be careful goin' up through Texas Canyon. It's gettin' purty western out there!"

Joe was unfamiliar with Texas Canyon and he got a kick out of this. It sounded like a line right out of one of his favorite cowboy movies. My father talked to Joe about reconsidering our plans to drive to Tucson that night and he confirmed that it would be dangerous through Texas Canyon, an area right outside of Willcox with roller coaster type hills and huge rock formations on either side of the interstate.

Joe made me promise not to tell anyone that we had stayed at the Comfort Inn, in Willcox, on our wedding night. What made it even better was that the room was given as a wedding gift from a college boyfriend. Of course, it was meant for one of our guests at our reception, but everyone had already made arrangements. Joe was so embarrassed about it, but I thought it was hysterical. After what we had been through, none of the opposition seemed terribly important at that moment. It seemed like we had had to climb a treacherous mountain to get to our wedding day and all that mattered was that we made it to the top!

I changed out of my wedding dress at my house. Not even thinking about how things were supposed to be, we crossed the threshold of the hotel room in jeans. We just stared at each other for a while, both feeling a little overwhelmed with our new reality.

"Well how does it feel to be Mrs. Joseph Oliver Reed III?"

"Did we really just get married? It seemed like a

dream."

"This is no dream, Mrs. Reed, and you just better get used to that name cuz it's yours forever!" We kissed and gazed at each other and smiled. We had kept the rules and now it was time to throw that rule book out the door. Thick snowflakes fell outside, covering the desert with a brilliant white we wouldn't appreciate until morning.

As we drove to Tucson the next day, the snow covered every cactus, bobbed wire fence, rock, and mountain in the distance. We couldn't stop smiling. We were really married and on our way to our first home. We stayed one night at the Hilton before flying to Georgia, in the place where we were originally booked for our special night. But of course, every night was special now.

Two days after getting married, we flew into Atlanta where Joe had his Berretta waiting. I had new scenery to marvel at as Joe drove us to our new home close to Ft. Benning. I had never seen so many vines. The lush green leaves blanketed every tree that lined the highway. A honeymoon? That would have to wait. Joe had to begin his officer training course the next morning.

Our little one bedroom apartment was furnished because we had nothing to our name. I didn't even know what "dowry" meant! It looked like it had been decorated in the '70s. A futon sofa and chair with a lovely metal pipe framing, a square of wicker accenting the sides with pale brown and rust plaid cushions greeted us as we opened the door. I was especially fond of the big orange and green flowered wall paper covering the bathroom walls. So it wasn't stylish, but it was our own place and we were together and that was all that mattered.

"And we lived happily ever after..." That's the way the story, goes doesn't it?

CHAPTER 9

You Don't Get Over It,
You Have to Go Through It!

The kids and I didn't officially move into our new Florida home until the end of November when most of our things were unpacked, furniture was arranged, and the blinds were covering every window. I needed that time to get used to the idea of being alone with my three young children. I'm grateful to my in-laws for letting me ease into my new life. I sat on the couch Joe and I had recently picked out. It had big fat "Army blue" (not navy blue) and white stripes. I fed Jessica while J.R. and Jasmine ran and danced and jumped around their new home. I let them have their moment while I had mine. I listened to their screams and laughter while I held Jessica and thought about where I was. I still couldn't believe how my life had changed since last April.

I had a reality check, something I continued to need to do now. *Joe died. He's in heaven. I'm a widow. I'm a mother of three. I live in Florida. Really? Yes, it's all true, Darla. Father in Heaven, please help me do this. Joe, you better help me as much as you can!*

Tears flowed and I felt a huge sob coming on, so I stopped all that thinking and yelled for my two miniature athletes to race back to me, "5...4...3...2..." and they came crashing in for a screaming group hug.

"Let's call someone and tell them about our new house!" More screaming. "Who do you wanna call, J.R.?"

He didn't hesitate with an answer, "Grampa!"

"Good idea!" I needed to talk to my parents about their trip out to Florida the next week, and I wanted to get all their flight information.

"Grampa, guess what! We have a new house!" J.R. walked back to his room with the phone. I could hear him describing every detail of his "101 Dalmatians" bedroom to my father. This was out of character for J.R. He really didn't like talking on the phone for very long but that night he jabbered away as he walked around the house with his grandpa in tow. I had to finally ask him if I could have my turn.

We held our first family prayer in our new home that night. It was another moment of realizing it was all up to me now.

Two days later, Monday morning, I received a phone call from Mom. I expected to hear my mother's cheerful voice, but instead I heard a "something's wrong" voice.

I put Jessica down so I could hear her better, "What's the matter, Mom?"

She answered in a very calm, monotone voice, "Your father just had a heart attack and he is gone."

He is gone? Gone to the hospital? Gone where?, I thought as I waited for her to finish the sentence. That was it. Dad was gone. She said she'd call back a little later. She still needed to call my other siblings.

I was in shock all over again, "Who's next!?" I asked the heavens.

I called my mother-in-law to let her know. Then my brother, Dennis called. We cried together. My father-in-law seemed to show up so quickly. I was grateful. He must have left what he was doing immediately to come be with me. Jessica was crying by now from being left in the crib so Pop helped me by soothing her while I talked. Dennis was able to explain what had happened. Dad had played basketball that morning. One of the men he played with said that he was showing off and shooting with his left hand because his right arm was hurting. He was, of course, making most of his shots. After he came home he talked to Mom for awhile and then went into the kitchen. That is when Mom heard a loud noise and went in to find him on the floor. She tried to do CPR when she saw he wasn't breathing, and then she called their doctor, who had just been playing basketball with Dad. He wasn't able to bring him back. He said his heart just stopped.

God took the two most important men in my life. Why? Flowers started arriving, people bringing food, and again I felt like others were moving too fast. I didn't want to do this again.

I called my Willcox therapist to know how to approach this with J.R. Victoria suggested asking him what he wanted to do. J.R. chose not to go to Arizona. I think it would've been too much reality for his little four-year-old heart to take and he knew it. I took Jasmine with me, and left J.R. and Jessica with Mamie and Pop.

I thought seeing Dad was going to help me accept his death. I was never able to see Joe, and I regretted not demanding to at least hold his hand one last time. So, with my father, I not only was able to look but I held his hand and touched, for the last time, his special finger. His right forefinger was missing the top section because as a young child he had a lawn mower accident. We enjoyed teasing him when he pointed, because he pointed with both his first and second finger, making it look like he was making a rude sign. In turn he used that finger to pop us in the head when we were misbehaving. It was part of who he was. It was part of so many fun memories.

I'm glad I touched Dad's hand. But as time went by, I realized that it was still hard for my mind to accept that my father had died. Seeing and touching him hadn't made it easier. This fact ruined my theory that if I would've seen Joe, it would have changed the way I grieved. Death is hard to deal with no matter what the situation; one moment they are a part of your life and the next they are not. For a time I even wondered what my faith did for me. I was grateful to know Joe was happy and busy and God had a darn good reason for taking him. I was grateful to know we'd be together again but it seemed for a time that all my faith did for me was help me look forward to my own death more than the next person. And my life seemed so incredibly long. I used to think that knowing about God and His plan for me could make everything easier. I didn't think anything this bad could happen to us if we were keeping all of God's commandments. On my mission I knew the answer to the question, "Why is life so hard?" When people would ask me, I would answer with a smile, "Life is a test. We are here to learn and grow and the challenges we face will help us to progress." I'd like to slap that clueless chick now! That was not so easy to take now that my sadness was so profound, and my "test" so hard and endless! My belief in Christ did not take the pain away. I was still feeling all the sadness of my husband's death. Looking to the future without Joe was beyond what I should be asked to do! I didn't feel prepared for this type of test and I didn't want to become strong!

I started going to a therapist. He teared-up as I told him my story. I didn't expect that. I guess I figured my story wasn't any sadder than the many stories he heard on a daily basis. It made me feel better to know he sympathized with me. He said I had a case of clinical depression and he could prescribe medication. This idea didn't appeal to me at all. I wanted to grieve. I didn't want to cover it up or pretend nothing was wrong. I started reading books about the stages of grief. I think I moved from numb to sad to angry in a very short time span. I was really angry with God for taking my best friend and for taking away my happy life. I still understood that God had a purpose in taking my husband and my father. I knew I could not comprehend His ways, and I still prayed and showed reverence for Him and pled for help. But I needed to be angry. I even had to stop going to therapy because I felt like the therapist was trying to hurry me through the anger stage—and that made me angry!

I would go to church angry that Joe wasn't on the stand conducting the meeting, teaching the Sunday school lesson, or giving the talk. He would have done a better job. I was angry that nobody there knew what an exceptional person my husband was. I was angry when women complained about their husbands or when they told me they were going out with their husbands or when they said anything about their husbands. I didn't want to see any couples with their arms around each other or rubbing each others backs during sacrament meeting (communion.) I wanted to announce, "This is worship service, not massage therapy!" I was also angry when people would share their "trials and tribulations," most of them seemed so trivial to me. I would think, "I win! Don't even try to compete with me! My trial beats all of yours put together!"

I was also angry when people would say, "How are you?" as they passed by. I wanted so badly to yell, "WELL IF YOU REALLY WANTED TO KNOW, YOU WOULD STOP AND WAIT FOR AN ANSWER, WOULDN'T YOU?!!"

Of course I would never be so obnoxious. Therefore, I would refuse to answer the question. I would just say, "Hi" or I would say quietly to myself as they passed by, "I'm overwhelmed with sadness and you?" I knew it was just a greeting, not a real question. But I needed it to be a question, and I needed them to wait and look at me and want to hear the answer.

I was grateful for good friends and family who would listen to me and would let me be angry. I am grateful to my friend, Michele. I told her that I was feeling guilty for being so angry and throwing fits. When I was frustrated with the kids or with my life in general I would hit walls, doors, cabinets. Sometimes I would make a dent or crack or the cabinet would fall apart. She shared that one week she had asked for her daughter's help every day, and that weekend she needed her daughter to baby sit the younger children. Her daughter proceeded to throw a fit, complaining about how unfair it was. She had plans and her mother had asked too much of her. Michelle said she just listened to her and couldn't disagree. She knew she had asked a lot of her that week, and she felt sympathy and love for her as she let her daughter throw this fit. She then said she was sure Heavenly Father had even more love and patience and sympathy than she possessed. She said He must look on with love and concern, knowing that what He has asked of me is extremely hard and He has let me throw my fit.

So why did I continue to go to church with all this anger? I still managed to be inspired by most lessons and talks and I received little answers to the questions I had in my heart. "How will the Lord make it up to me? How am I supposed to get through this? How can I contain my anger and be patient with the children?" Staying home was not an option. I'm grateful to my parents for forming this habit I just couldn't break. I have tried to do the same for my children. Attending and participating consistently helped me to build a brand new faith in God, as my conditional, superficial faith was stripped away.

There were many in my ward who reached out to me. The very first time I took the children to church I was so nervous. I wondered how the heck I was going to take care of all three of them by myself. J.R. was four, Jasmine was 21 months and Jessica was two months. I didn't know anyone, so I knew I wouldn't get help. I just prayed I would be able to handle it. Not long into the meeting a teenage girl sat down by me and immediately asked if she could hold my baby. I immediately offered a prayer of thanks. Mary, my new teenage angel, sat by me week after week, helping with the children. They loved her and I will always love her.

Cathy, who was the president of the Primary (the children's group in the church) would call and ask if she could take my girls for awhile. "My girls" sounds easy but remember that my girls consisted of a toddler and a small baby! This alone time was precious to me. I wanted to be able to sit still for a moment. The world was still moving much too quickly for me. I felt like I was being pulled along, like a person walking a huge dog is pulled. That's what I pictured when I thought about the uncomfortable pace I was being forced to take. The person is leaning back with their feet hitting the pavement heavily as they resist the fast pace. I felt like I was always pulling back on that leash, trying to slow it down! I was so grateful to Cathy for giving me small breaks from this forced fast pace.

My mother and father-in-law, better known as Mamie and Pop, were an incredible support, along with Daria and Vonda. They not only took care of the children when I needed help, but they loved them (and still do) with more energy than I've ever seen in grandparents or aunts. It was a celebration when we would arrive, like they hadn't seen the kids in years.

Mamie would throw her hands up and exclaim, "Oh my Jazzy and my J.R. are here... and baby Jess-i-ca!" They would hold them, talk to them, and get on the floor to play with them. When Jessi would cry, Pop would hold her in front of the big mirror in their dining room and talk to her as she looked at their image. This usually calmed her down quickly. I know she was listening intently to what he had to say.

They also would put the children "in the spotlight." Their stage was a little stool or the fire place hearth, with a candelabrum as their microphone. They would introduce them like they were performing at the Grammy awards, "Introducing, all the way from North Carolina, the very talented and beautiful, Jasmine Alexandria Reed!"

Applause and cheering would continue until she walked around the corner and stepped up on her stage to perform. A dance, a song, a story—whatever she did would get cheers and hugs and praise. My children knew they were the center of the universe!

I have a video of Jasmine I taped when she was three years old. She had become such an accomplished actress that I was having her pretend she was sad, and then happy, scared, and angry, and when I said, "Now be shy," she responded with, "wha, wha, what's shy, Mommy?" This question describes her perfectly. I give so much credit to my in-laws who continued to help my children feel at-home on center stage.

Jessica had a second baby shower in Florida. Mamie really knows how to throw a party! We didn't play the normal little baby shower games we are all accustomed to. She had women competing with a set of jacks, a paddle ball, and jump rope. She also had the whole group do the "macarena". The porch was filled with woman dancing and celebrating the arrival of this new little precious girl. I'm so grateful to Mamie and her dear friends who showed so much love to me at such a debilitating time in my life.

Our relationship had definitely changed through the years. I would sometimes think back and be amazed with the turn of events. Mamie would say that it was meant to be, that I was chosen to raise these children.

Remembering the first time I talked to Joe's mom after we were married makes me cringe. I asked Joe if I should call her by her first name and he advised me not to even ask! I had been working with women of all ages at the health club and had friends who were much older than me, whom I called by their first name. In the West or at least in Arizona this was acceptable. Calling her Mrs. Reed seemed so cold and formal. I didn't think it was right to address my mother-in-law in that way. So I didn't listen to Joe and proceeded to ask her if I could call her by her first name. Joe was waving his hands in protest, but I thought I knew better. His mother said she would prefer that I call her Mrs. Reed. In my mind she was letting me know that she wasn't ready to accept me as family.

Now, many years later, after living in the South, I wish I would have listened to Joe that day. It now sounds wrong when children address me by my first name. It is definitely a cultural and a regional thing. Joe used to think that once his family met me, I would "charm their socks off!" I really blew my first chance. Actually I'm pretty sure they all still have their socks on nice and tight!

The Sunday after we were married, Joe and I were excited to attend church together. I was extremely proud of Joe and happy that we were finally together after all we had been through. I thoroughly enjoyed having Joe introduce us as husband and wife. I thought it went quite well. Joe later said he could hear the air sucked out of the chapel when we walked in. I guess I was in my own little happy, oblivious world. I think it was more the older generation who might have been doing the gasping. I have nothing but good memories of our time in that ward.

My mother's vision of skin heads and burning crosses never came about. The worst we noticed were heads turning, stares, and raised eyebrows. We just smiled and kept going. We didn't pay them no neva' mind!

For the Martin Luther King Jr. celebration, we went to Atlanta. I was thrilled to be surrounded by so many beautiful black people. Joe kept telling me to stop staring but I was in awe of the many different braided hair styles. He let me know that he was getting glares from quite a few black women, and after he clued me in I started to notice.

I wanted to stand up on my soap box and say, "Hey, how can you be upset about us? WE ARE the "dream" that Marten Luther King Jr. had! You should put us on one of your floats!"

We enjoyed the parade, and especially loved the bands. I wished I could've been part of a band like that, "throwin' down" as they marched up the street. It was so far from my little hometown "fighting cowboys" band, moving into the W-formation as we played "On Wisconsin."

Our first year of marriage was wonderful and difficult. We were trying to get used to each other. Joe was "in the field" for a week every few weeks and I was trying to figure out what to do with myself. I was very dependent upon him for my happiness, not a healthy way to be. I got my feelings hurt easily and I would run to the room and cry. Sometimes he would leave to take a drive. He needed alone time. I wanted to talk everything out. I got a couple traffic tickets in just a few months, my first traffic tickets ever, I might add. Joe was angry and I felt like a child in trouble.

We received no toaster for a wedding gift and we tortured ourselves by going months without one. Oven-burnt toast was a norm for breakfast. He said I fooled him good, making him think I could cook. That was on account of our first picnic at PepsiCo Park when I made fried chicken, potato salad, pork and beans and homemade chocolate chip cookies. I did cook all of that myself, but I just couldn't seem to duplicate that meal those first few months.

At one point I remember thinking, "Now I understand why people get divorced: the happily-ever-after thing actually takes a lot of work, i.e.: unselfishness, being careful about what you say, and swallowing your pride." The thing that helped us was our love for each other and our commitment to each other and to God. Forever was the plan and we were both determined. If we didn't talk things out earlier in the day, by the time we were ready to go to bed someone started the apologies because we didn't want to go to bed angry. We couldn't be upset with each other when we knelt down together, side by side, hand in hand, by our bed. Every night, without fail, we prayed together before going to sleep. It was a humbling moment. It helped us to realize that our goal was to follow the Lord's example on how to treat each other, and that loving each other was going to take a little extra effort some days.

I found little jobs here and there. I worked for a temp agency and I took a college course, French literature, which lead me to jobs with language camps over the summer. Our church group kept me busy too. I taught early morning seminary and I really loved my small group of six kids. They also had me lead the music in church and be the choir director. This was hysterical because I had no idea what I was doing! One time we sang "The Battle Hymn of the Republic," as a choir. I had a great version of that hymn by the Tabernacle Choir on cassette tape. I didn't have the sheet music for the different arrangement so we just mimicked the "Tab" with our bass singing an extra "truth is marching, truth is marching." We sounded just as good as the Tab that day, or so I thought. I enjoyed pretending I was a great director.

Joe started Ranger School in June. I still don't quite understand what possesses a man to go through such rigorous training. I was in awe of what my husband put himself through for that little Ranger Tab. He explained as he would always be in leadership positions, it was important to be the example. He knew it would help him be a better infantryman.

During some phases of training they were only allowed to eat one meal a day and have two hours of sleep. They planned missions, marched, climbed and rappelled mountains, and jumped out of planes. All the while, they had someone yelling at them to quit, "Give up Ranger! You know you wanna go home!"

To make things harder, he was dealing with an ankle injury that hadn't healed. I would've been crying like a baby on the first day. The fact that Joe made it through this type of test of strength and endurance of mind, body, and spirit, made my admiration and love for him grow.

It was supposed to last two months and every

two weeks they would get about nine hours to wash clothes, eat, and sleep. Through letters or quick occasional phone privileges, he would give me specific instructions as to what to bring when I picked him up.

...The plan is this - I don't want to eat all at once and not junk food! So please when you show up have a homemade pizza ready in the car. Also bring some civilian clothes for me to wear along with my Nike flip-flops and white G's (underwear.)

...Oh, by the way the jump was great, though I got a little sick in the air. <u>HE</u> really does answer prayer.

...By the time you get this I will be on one MRE a day!

I picked him up with the homemade pizza in the car. I drove us to the PX to get more supplies and as I pulled into the parking lot the pizza was gone! It was a large and thick pizza and he downed the whole thing in about fifteen minutes! I had a Cornish hen, mashed potatoes and gravy meal for him when we got home. He downed that in record time as well. I just watched in amazement. I was then ready for some attention from my husband but once his head hit the pillow he was out. I had never seen anyone sleep so hard, snoring as he inhaled and exhaled!

Joe said that during Ranger School he didn't hear any nasty stories or talk of women at all. Instead, the conversation was about food and sleep! He recalled Maslow's "hierarchy of needs" he had learned about at West Point and thought it was cool to be able to see the theory proven first hand. The physiological needs came first!

During the Florida swamp phase of training he called me to let me know that he had been "recycled", which meant he didn't pass that particular phase and would have to wait two weeks and do the two week phase again. This added another month to our separation. I remember crying after hanging up with him. He was the one who should've been boo-hooing! He did get a break but had to stay in Florida, so I drove to Ft. Myers, to see him. He told me we were going to get a temporary housing apartment to stay in, so I cooked a huge meal and brought it with me. But once I arrived, I found out there weren't any openings on Post and Joe couldn't go off Post. Our amazing dinner I had planned was ruined. That night I had to stay in a nasty little motel by myself. I had another good cry.

My Dearest Darla,

I just wanted to write you and apologize for our not getting a room today. I know you went out of your way to make our time together special. I am sorry I seemed so unaffected by it all, but I have grown used to things going sour on me after extensive plans have been made. But Darls, anytime I am with you is special for me. Right now the situation is not the greatest. But you know as well as I that we've survived worse than this and for longer periods of time. I need you to be as strong as you can and not let this all get you down. …. I know this is kinda corny but here's a Ranger tab for you to put in your wallet to help keep you focused on the goal here. I figure if we both look forward to graduation and getting the tab the better both our attitudes will be. … I love you babes and in about 1 month I'll have a Ranger Tab and be home with my favorite girl. …

Loving you forever,

Joe

This letter not only helped me then, it speaks to me now, as his widow. "Be as strong as you can, focus on the goal sweetheart," I hear him saying to me. The Ranger Tab is a motivating symbol, a symbol of extraordinary strength and endurance. During that first year without him I was on a roller coaster of emotions as I tried to endure each day. I would go from angry, to sad, to inspired, and back to angry again. His little notes from Ranger School reminded me of the big picture. I had a job to do. As hard as it was, I needed to do the best I could. I would tell myself, "Suck it up and drive on, Ranger!" I would wear his Ranger shirt when I was out mowing the lawn and doing other jobs that I thought Joe would have done, and it made me feel "hooah!" I learned this word at our first welcome assembly for IOBC at Ft. Benning. As they showed a video of soldiers jumping out of planes and participating in combat and rappelling I heard a barking type noise coming from the crowd, Joe later translated, "hooah." It has multiple meanings. A person is "hooah" when he or she is tough or has good character. You say "hooah" to say "yes," or to say "I agree with what you said," or to cheer someone on. You can also say it whenever the mood hits you! I felt like I was going through a type of Ranger School and I had to be tough. I had to be "hooah" and work hard for the ultimate Ranger Tab from God.

My first Christmas after Joe died was painful,

though having it with his family made it a little more bearable. We were all struggling with our emotions. It helped to be able to share in the excitement the children had for this magical day. They were feeling pure happiness and it was contagious.

Our anniversary came the next week. I naturally wanted to go to the temple but was heartbroken to find out it was closed for Christmas break. So I did the next best thing— retail therapy. Mamie took the children that day, as she continued to do on most difficult days. Someone sent me a beautiful bouquet of white roses. I called everyone I knew and they all refused to fess up. I wanted to know who to thank, but in not having anybody else's name associated with them, it was easier to imagine them being from Joe. The white roses had a heavenly glow to them as if they came straight from his new home.

Then came Valentines Day! Heartache was a more meaningful word to me. My heart literally, physically, ached. Even though I was given more than what Joe would have given me: roses from my family, chocolates and a flower from Mamie, and a box of French chocolate cookies from my friend, Cathy.

My journal entry:

Dear Joe,　　　　　　　　　　　　*Feb. 1997*

Your little boy is having a rough time. I think he's feeling anger just like me. As we left the fitness club, the girls at the counter said, "Give mommy and daddy a valentine kiss." J.R. yelled back at them "I don't have a daddy!" That hurt so much babes. I quickly said, "J.R. you have a daddy, he's in heaven." He returned with "My daddy is not here!"

I've heard quite a few analogies to the situation I've been thrown into. One is comparing a tragedy like this to planning a trip to Italy and ending up in Holland. Holland seems too pretty. I think it should be a little more drastic, like the difference between the Bahamas and Antarctica. That's something that would really throw you off, you've packed swimsuits, shorts, and light weight clothes, you planned on 80 degree weather and now you are in 40 below. OK, deal with it!!!

My favorite analogy though is if your right arm was cut off!! That's how dysfunctional I feel right now. Yes, eventually I'll get used to living without my right arm. People try to comfort me by saying "now your left arm is going to *get so much stronger!" Oh joy, that's something to get excited about. And of course I have my death to look forward to because then I will have my right arm once again! That is a blessing and I'm grateful for that promise, but here I am with quite a few years to go (I think) in this life without my right arm. The challenges before me seem endless. Everyday duties seem to overwhelm me. The responsibilities of raising 3 children without my right arm are beyond my abilities. The way I'm dealing with it? Having a good cry daily seems to help, prayers for strength, and I take one day at a time.*

I am grateful for all the help I've received. Your family is so loving and supportive. Mamie watches the children for me quite a bit, and Vonda is slowly moving in, she's a great help and I'm enjoying being able to talk with her.

After Valentines Day came Joe's birthday, which is also the anniversary of the day we first met. To make it a special day I had some friends meet me at the temple and we did work for his ancestors. I knew it was a party Joe would attend. I usually tried to plan something on those special days so that I wouldn't be home sobbing. I took it a day at a time and I continued to find solace in his journals and letters. I found some kind of message from him in all his letters as I went through the most difficult days, but I didn't expect his Ranger notes to inspire me as they did. "Drive on Ranger, drive on…"

Joe passed the Florida phase the second time around and went on to the desert phase in Dugway, Utah. The last month of Ranger School seemed to go by faster. I stayed busy and my attitude changed a bit, carrying the Ranger Tab in my wallet helped.

I love you Darls and although we're apart you are always my 1ˢᵗ concern. ….keep driving on at the home front and remember that I'll always love you no matter what happens with Ranger School, the Army or any of this stuff. You are what matters most to me and I will not let you down.

As he was finishing his last phase in Ranger School, the news was filled with "Desert Shield." I watched from outside my apartment as twenty or so buses drove out of town. Their loved ones lined the interstate, waving flags. Hundreds of yellow ribbons were tied to every pole, tree, and bush. I was grateful Joe was not a passenger on any of those buses but I was afraid that he would soon be.

Fri. 11 Aug. 90

...I suppose you know about the crisis in the Middle East and the troops getting pulled out. Thus far in my platoon alone we've had 4 people taken out of Ranger school because their unit is being deployed. A lot of my bud's from school and IOBC have already gone, I don't think the 1st Infantry Division, Ft. Riley has been called up yet so don't you worry just yet.

I did worry, but I didn't let myself actually accept that my husband would go to war, that couldn't happen to us! I had been sheltered as a child. War seemed like something that only happened long ago. I couldn't fathom such an experience being mine.

Joe graduated from Ranger School and I was honored to pin his Ranger Tab on him. Before he started, three months earlier, his body was one of an athlete: v-shaped, ripped abs, broad, muscular arms and chest. After Ranger School, after he had starved himself then binged, then starved again, his body had totally changed. He had a pencil neck, chubby chipmunk cheeks, a protruding stomach, small arms, and no lat's. The v-shape was now an A. *Where did my husband go?* He already had a work-out plan devised to get him back to normal. He was much more disturbed about his physical state than I was.

For at least a month after Ranger School I had to drive because he would fall asleep at any given moment, usually right in the middle of a conversation—sometimes while he was talking! He also continued to eat like he was still in Ranger School, being deprived of food. I watched in awe as he would down his food like he hadn't eaten in days. He used to have such impeccable manners!

CHAPTER 10

Storms Will Come

Not long after his return we were watching the evening news and there was an announcement of all the units that were being deployed. Ft. Riley, Kansas, the "Big Red One" was called off along with others. This was where Joe was going after his Bradley training. That was it! That was our notification. That was how we found out Joe would be going to fight in a war! I thought there should be an official form in the mail, or a call from Ft Riley. No, nothing but the 5 o'clock news. I felt sick.

This was in August, and we found out he would be leaving late December. We were grateful for the time we had, though it seemed to be a time for our anxiety to build. We did have some nice distractions. His parents were having their 25th wedding anniversary, and this would be my debut as Joe's wife with his family and friends.

As we were greeted at their front door, it seemed like nothing had ever been wrong. Mr. and Mrs. Reed greeted me with a smile and welcomed me into their home. The only disappointment was when we were told where we would sleep. I was in a twin bed in a room with one of his sisters and he was on the floor in the family room. This was a clue that they were not yet thrilled about us being married! But I wasn't bitter. I just joined my husband on the floor after everyone else went to sleep, thank you very much!

I was still uneasy the night of the party. Joe's family is so beautiful. I had a black velvet Liz Claiborne dress I felt confident in but I still felt inadequate and awkward in their presence. I had never gone to a party this fancy before. It was more elegant than our wedding reception. Everyone was dressed in black-tie attire. Joe was so happy. It was good to see the tension between him and his family now over.

Joe completed a Bradley Vehicle training course and then we prepared to move. We had some things sent to Arizona, where I would live while he was gone, and the rest was placed in storage. We were told he would be deployed for up to a year. We drove all the way to Arizona at the end of December to spend Christmas with my family. Though we had a wonderful time seeing everyone, it was hard to have Christmas joy when we knew what was coming. Joe could hardly eat, his nerves were so bad.

From Arizona, we drove up to Kansas and stayed in temporary housing while we waited for the day he would leave. The date they originally gave us was just after Christmas but the date continued to be pushed back, so we were blessed to have more time. Although it was a bittersweet celebration, we were actually able to spend our first anniversary together.

The date of deployment came shortly after. They were to report at night. I don't remember the time but I remember the darkness. That day Joe had given me a blessing. He had helped me to understand more deeply the importance of his holding the priesthood. He did not take it for granted. He tried to live his life so that he could always be worthy to give blessings, whether someone was sick or needed comfort or words of wisdom from above. I'd never had a blessing like this touch me as much as this one did. It was as if the Lord was speaking directly to me through my husband. He promised me that he would return safely from the war and we would have children and I would be strengthened while he was away. After the blessing, we held each other and sobbed.

Watching the news when it's covering a deployment always brings me to tears. I cry for them as well as for myself as I remember. I didn't want to stop holding him and kissing him as we said goodbye. I cried myself to sleep every night as the realization sunk in that my husband had gone to war. It was more than I could fathom.

The blessing Joe had given me kept me from worrying as much. I knew he would not be killed, but I didn't know if he would not be seriously injured. I also had anxiety over him having to kill someone and someone trying to kill him. A couple days after I said goodbye to Joe, Dennis flew up to Kansas and drove back to Arizona with me. I will always be grateful for the sacrifices my brother has made for me! I went back to the job I had before I was married. Being a personal trainer and talking to women all day helped me to not be as overwhelmed with what my husband was doing. I also took a biology class at the community college. It was good I stayed busy and couldn't stay glued to the news all day. My sister, Danette, lived close by and she helped keep me busy also.

My Most Dear Darla,　　　　*Jan. 1991*

Right now I am somewhere over the Atlantic Ocean between New York and Rome. We flew from Topeka to New York City, where we refueled and got a new crew. Our next stop is Rome, Italy, where this letter will be mailed from. Anyways the most remarkable thing just happened! I was contemplating writing you a letter and asking a Flight attendant to mail it for me, when out of the blue a Flight Attendant gives me this paper and an envelope and says that she'll get my letter mailed in Rome!! ☺ I about flipped! Darla can I tell you that I am very very scared right now. My hands have been shaking ever since I last saw you. All I can think about is you and coming home to start my family. I have read my patriarchal Blessing 3 times now in the past few hours. It is an extreme comfort to me, though I'm still afraid. Every few minutes I find myself choking back tears that should have been cried a long time ago. I've also been reading my scriptures and for "some reason" my hunger for the words of the Savior have increased ten fold. It is amazing to see how I'm changing already (how my heart is changing)! Well I guess it is not a change but more of a recommitment to do as I should.

As I think back now on how I teased

you about being weak I can see that I am the weak one, because I did not have the strength and courage to commit myself to daily scripture study as you have counseled me to do. And I'm not being hard on myself, it is the truth and you know it. Darla, if I said all the wonderful things about you it would not take me all night it would take me a life time; so that is what I'm going to set out to do because Darla Fay Reed I love you and I'm going to do everything in my power to take you to the celestial kingdom!!!

Now as soon as I get to Saudi I'm going to start making you your first tape so I need you to send me some of those small padded packages to mail them in. I'll also need plenty of stamps.

So how was your drive home with Dennis? Pleasant I hope! I trust that you are getting settled in okay? If you need help from someone get it. Oh yeah please tell Dennis I extend my warmest thanks for his offering and willingness to drive home with you. He's a good man!! And I'm glad he's my brother-in-law.

Alright Sweetheart, next stop Rome! Someday you and I will visit here under more favorable conditions!

Love you eternally,

Joey

Joe's journal:

11 January 1991

I could not sleep again last night. CPT Williams snored half of the night so it was not exactly quiet. I got up around 0230 and listened to some tapes. Then I decided to go ahead and read my scriptures in the latrine since I couldn't sleep.

I was reading in the Book of Mosiah where King Limhi took his people up to battle against the Lamanites; and I was impressed at how he always referred to going to battle "in the strength of the Lord"! As I reflected on my own situation here in Saudi Arabia I can see definite parallels. King Limhi had to rely on the Lord's strength and not that of he and his people. For if he had not trusted and exercised complete faith on the Lord the Lamanites would have surely crushed he and his smaller nation. Along the same lines, I am going to have to increase my faith and put my trust in the Lord or else I will surely fail at the task before me. I as a new Lieutenant have been given a platoon of 28 men and 4 Bradley Fighting Vehicles and told that I must lead them in War. I have virtually no experience in a Bradley much less leading a platoon of them, I have never worked with my men and they have almost no reason to trust me or my abilities, and most of all I am scared myself!!!!! I only pray that the Lord will bless me to develop quickly and help me to do those things that will keep both me and my men alive.

My brother, Dale, came home from his mission and lived in my little apartment with me. Joe had written Dale before he finished his mission and had asked him to live with me so he wouldn't have to worry as much. It was great to have that time with my little brother. He is just three years younger than I and we teased and fought and laughed all through high school.

One incident stands out in my mind. Early one morning, we were on our way to seminary, a scripture study class before school. It started at 7:00 AM, but we were late, and I was annoyed. As I drove the short distance in our station wagon, one of my favorite songs came on. Because we lived in a small town, I had to get the "good music" on an AM station that didn't come in very well. There was a little static but I turned it up and was singing along. "Nobody's gonna' break my stride, nobody's gonna slow me down…oh no…I've got to keep on movin'." Suddenly the song was covered with loud static. Dale had turned the car vent up as high as it would go so he could blow dry his hair. I turned the vent off. He turned it on. I turned it off. He turned it on, turned the radio off, took the radio knob off and threw it in the back of the station wagon! I went ballistic! Listening to that song right then was the most important thing in the world! I pulled over, climbed over the seats, retrieved the knob, replaced it where it belonged, turned my music back on, turned the vent off and somewhere in between all that I managed to slap him on the back. We had a moment of silent glaring at each other as I was panting from my little work-out, and then he busted out laughing. That was my brother. He dealt with my big sister bossiness with a sense of humor and we were never angry with each other for long.

He left on his mission to England just a few months before I came home from mine so we hadn't seen each other for almost three and a half years. The last time I saw him, he was a boy. I couldn't stop staring at this man who looked like my little brother. I would randomly approach him and say, "You're a man!" And he would say, "Yes, yes I am."

He still had that great sense of humor which I needed. I liked how he prayed. He was very specific with God, "Please help the small amount of milk we have to be sufficient for our cereal this morning…"

Joe's phone privileges were few and far between so I never knew exactly when the call would come, but I became accustomed to it being him when the phone rang at two or three in the morning.

I would jump out of bed, half out of it and shaking from the surprise alarm, rambling as soon as I picked up the phone: "Joe, I love you so much I miss you what is going on out there where are you I got your letter are you okay...?"

"Darla!" he would have to interrupt. He always had important things he had to tell me concerning taxes or our credit card or maintenance on the Beretta.

We only had about 10 minutes and his side of the conversation reflected the pressure he felt from a line of soldiers behind him waiting their turn. Our short communication always left me frustrated and anxious but grateful to have heard his voice and know that he was all right.

Joe's journal:

18 Jan 91

Yesterday at 0200 in the morning the United States launched an air attack against the forces of Saddam Hussein in Kuwait and Iraq. About that time the whole compound, MGM, was alerted to the possibility of a SCUD missile attack. Someone came bursting into our room yelling for us to get into our MOPP gear and to take an anti nerve agent pill. Between myself, Kevin Hub, Rob Mitchell and the commander CPT Williams our room took on a much different atmosphere than we had established earlier in the week. Fortunately we all reacted correctly and packed our things in the event of evacuation. After we had packed all of our things the warning came down as a possible SCUD attack and we all jumped into action by masking and moving to a lower floor of our building. About this time I finally got those feelings that one might have when his life is in imminent danger. Suddenly the realization of an actual war starting and me being in it was upon me. I'm glad to say that my first thoughts were those of my platoon and its well being, but I was quickly comforted with the thoughts that SFC Barksdale was a capable Platoon Sergeant that could deal with the situation. Then I thought of my beloved wife, Darla, and how she would take all of this. Surely the American Media was all over the first attack which would be broadcasted across the world. I didn't have to wonder about Mom & Dad. I knew that Dad would be in front of the T.V. and that Mom would be in tears.

The biggest comfort throughout this whole ordeal was my patriarchal Blessing. It continues to be a blessing and strength to me as the days go on. I humbly pray that when my time arrives that I will be able to do my duty in the strength of the Lord!

He had planned to call me that night at Danette's apartment. I watched the news as I waited for his call, not knowing exactly where he was and if he was affected by the attack. I didn't have the privilege of knowing what had happened until I received the letter from him much later.

After a couple months I found out that most photo copy stores let family members send faxes to their soldier for free. I kept him up to date with important things like: which team was ahead in the NCAA Final Four, what movies I had seen, and how much I missed and loved him. I still had to wait for snail mail from him but I cherished each letter and cassette tape I received. Besides reading his words, I could fall asleep at night soothed by the sound of his voice.

Joe's journal:

3 March 1991

It has been exactly one week since the Ground War began and 2-16 Infantry crossed from Saudi Arabia into Iraq. Right now we are sitting off a road in Iraq, securing it for when the military dignitaries go by to begin peace talks with the Iraqis. The talks should last between two and seven days. I'm fasting today that all will go well and an agreement can be made.

Last Sunday when we moved out from the south side of the brim I was lucky enough to receive 4 letters from Darla the night prior. I was definitely a happy soldier. That day however was full of anxiety and nervousness. It seems like it took forever to get to where the enemy was located. As we moved across the desert, the scene was one that epitomized the Army's doctrine of air land battle. As far as the eye could see were m-1 tanks, Bradley's, M13's, and attack helicopters just creeping across the desert waiting to strike the enemy. The only problem was that no enemy struck. All of a sudden out of the sand were men popping up with white flags. They were coming from all around, hundreds of POW's surrendering willfully and cheerfully. The first set of POW's we had to secure I had to take SSG Shaw's squad, a decision I reluctantly had to make. I'm sure those Iraqis were more afraid of us than we were of them, nevertheless it was our first time to handle POW's. I found myself having to yell a lot to get my men to move but they as well as I got rid of their initial fear. We had about nine of them that we thoroughly strip searched. I will never forget the look in their eyes as we searched them for weapons and any useful documents. Mostly there was fear, but they also were relieved from what must have been a horrible experience. Some of them had shoes (boots) others didn't, most of them had uniforms though they were all different kinds of patterns. They also had civilian clothes underneath their uniforms. All of them were sick and had lice. It was a fairly pathetic sight as we herded them like cattle, strip searched them and then corralled them for transport to the rear.

As the morning pressed on we easily handled over 100 POW's, and this was prior to getting to our objective.

At around 1500 we hit the trench system which was abandoned. There was nobody there however there were plenty of weapons and ammo. Since our mission was to destroy everything except low boys we commenced "firing up" bunkers, trenches, command posts, weapons etc. Later on in the day we encountered more POW's, which tied us up for the rest of the evening.

The following day we ended up clearing trench lines for about 8 km as well as handling a few more POW's. Our main mission was then complete and we settled back into a hasty defensive position and became the Corps reserve for two days. One hundred hours after the Ground War began Kuwait City had been liberated and Allied Forces occupied Southern Iraq. The President called for a cease fire and we began our two day move to this location.

On our way we passed by enemy graveyards where the Air Force had totally ripped apart Iraq's Elite Republican Guard Tanks. There were tanks totally demolished lying all over to include a few dead Iraqi bodies.

Just a few minutes ago Col Marino drove by with the delegation from Iraq to go to the Peace talks with Gen. Schwarzkopf. I honestly hope and pray that all goes well with these talks. I seriously want to get out of here and continue with my life.

In April, Joe let me know that he would be coming home soon and that I needed to plan on moving to Kansas, "It's time to get outa' dodge, Sweetheart!"

I decided I wanted to get myself moved into a place for us before he got home, so I prepared to leave Arizona. Dennis helped drive me back to Kansas, as far as Wichita where he could fly home. I felt a little nervous as I pulled out of the airport parking lot with a U-Haul in tow. I had a friend in Junction City, Chris, who I would stay with while I looked for a place. We had met through our husbands and I had stayed with her the night they left for Iraq.

Joe's journal:

5 March 1991

Yesterday, after moving back from our security position by the airfield where the peace talks were conducted, we (the company) got 'hey you'd' by battalion to go back to the airfield to act as route guides for Iraqi refugees fleeing from the rioting and chaos in Baghdad and Basra! Evidently the Republican Guard Troops of Iraq are punishing the people for not supporting them in the War.

Once we took up our position next to the airfield the convoy/caravans came pouring in. The people were stacked in cars, vans, trucks, anything that would move them. They smiled, and waved as they passed our positions. I cannot believe nor understand what it is they are going through. We Americans are sheltered from these realities in other parts of the world. We casually eat our ice cream and watch the 1800 news then pass the troubles of the world off as "oh well, sucks to be them!"

But as I watched the Iraqi children pass by in the cars and vans, I noticed the same familiar smile, laugh, and gleam in their eyes as American kids. For that manner they were the same as any child any where in the world, playful, curious, and loveable. Sometimes it is hard to comprehend how vast the kingdom of God really is until you've been around and seen all the many people that inhabit the earth. Tears came to my eyes once again as I looked at these good people with the *knowledge that they too are children of our Heavenly Father and that Christ lived and died to extend salvation unto their souls as well as anybody else in the world.*

By the time the day for them to return came, I had located an apartment, had our things sent to us which included some furniture from Joe's parents, and set up house. I was determined to give him the gift of having a real home to come home to.

Wives, children, and parents all waited anxiously in a hangar on Post. We probably waited at least an hour or so. Suddenly, the military band started playing, and the soldiers filed in. Flags were waving, and people were jumping up and down and cheering. After scanning dozens of soldiers filing in through a doorway, I saw my Joe. He was holding a carnation and when our eyes met, he gave me his biggest smile. As he got closer to me I was able to run up to him but only for a quick hug and kiss. He had to stay in line and get into formation. I wanted to yell, "Let me have my husband back now!" They only tortured us for a moment; after a little speech, they officially dismissed them.

"For after much tribulation, come the blessings." This LDS scripture seemed to describe that moment in time. Joe smiled as he walked into our new little apartment. I gave him a tour as he expressed his appreciation for all I had done to prepare for his homecoming. It was such a good feeling to be back together again, I couldn't stop staring at him and wanting to hold onto him and I prayed this little feeling of heaven would last.

I have thought many times of some women at the fitness club where I worked while Joe was serving in Desert Storm. They complained about their husbands, and were so bored with them that my situation appealed to them.

They joked, "Where can I sign him up?"

I never had the luxury of getting bored with my husband. I couldn't fathom it and I was hoping we wouldn't have any more long separations so I could see how that might feel.

All the letters he wrote me while he served in the Gulf War went into a box I quickly forgot about, I knew they were amazing love letters I would want to reread someday.

I didn't imagine that "some day" would come so soon, and I didn't imagine I would want to read and reread these letters so often. As the one year anniversary of his death approached, I ached to talk to my husband. I had been pleading with God to let him come to me. The first time Mamie and Pop took the kids all night I talked out loud to Joe and told him he could come for a visit now. Nothing happened. I've heard so many amazing stories of people who weren't even asking for a visitation but have had amazing experiences. What was wrong with me? Was I not worthy? One story I heard was about a man whose mother died in a horrible way. She was robbed and killed, and the son was tormented by the details of her death. One night the mother came to him in a dream and let her son know that the joy she felt now far exceeded the pain she felt when she died. I was comforted by this story as I was a bit tormented by the way Joe died, but I was also jealous! Why didn't Joe come to me? Why didn't I get a vision?

A few people shared with me their experiences with either dreaming of Joe or having a strong feeling of his presence. My sister, Danette, had an amazing dream on the airplane ride to North Carolina that morning after Joe died. As she was dozing off she saw Joe dressed in white and he spoke to her: "Everything will be all right. Take care of Darla and be a good example to my family." Amazing! I was grateful for this message from my husband. Years later, Joe's cousin Sonia, nicknamed "Neet", called me and shared with me a dream she had had. She was sitting on a beach and Joe came and sat down by her and told her to tell me that he loved me and that he would be there for me and his children. It was nice to know that he was still trying to get this message to me. Joe's friend Kevin said he had a couple experiences where he knew Joe was with him, once in his own home and once when he was in Joe's closet talking to J.R. about his dad. Why did they have these amazing experiences and why didn't I? Again, I was comforted by his experiences but I was also troubled because of my strong desire to have my own visit from Joe.

It was at about this time when the Army arranged a meeting with Pop and I to explain the details of the accident Joe was involved in. We didn't find out too much more than what we already knew. I don't know if I had been told before but this was the first time I became aware that Joe was the co-pilot. Three Kiowa Warrior helicopters were flying side by side over the Texas desert. They were supposed to fire ammunition and then go off to the right, one at a time. This was just before midnight and they all had night vision goggles on, which takes away their peripheral vision. After one helicopter fired their ammunition, the two remaining helicopters collided in air. Three men died that night and one walked away. One of the family members of another man who died contacted me to join him in questioning the Army on this incident. I didn't have the energy nor did I feel a need to. I really believe the verses in the Bible which teach us that our time on Earth is determined and appointed. I also believed that the blessing I received the day I was notified of his death was from God. I imagined that perhaps, when it is our time to go, God just calls off our guardian angels who are probably keeping us safe continuously, and they just let things happen. I came up with the idea that the military just makes it easier on God because something is bound to happen when you're either at war or practicing for war. All I knew for sure was that God was and is in charge and it was His will for Joe to be with Him.

I had many conversations with others about where my husband was and what he was doing. Some tried to convince me that Joe was much too busy to be hanging around my home. They were trying to convince me that I should "move on." I hate that phrase! So many people have asked me if I think I will be able to "move on." I know what they want to ask. They want to know if I'm going to date and marry again. Why don't they just ask what they want to know? Am I going to be able to put my life and my love for Joe behind me, someone I gave my whole heart to and committed not only this life but all eternity to and start a new life with someone else? Well, I like to ignore what they are getting at and say, "I 'moved on' the day after my husband was killed. I got up and I kept moving, and I have continued to 'move on' as I raise our children!"

I didn't like being told that Joe would want me to be with someone else. We never did have a conversation where he told me to marry someone else if he died. "Talk to me Babes," I would plead for him to come and tell me that he still cared for me and his children and that he would be close by as I raised them. I never did get a visitation, but each night, I would go to my special drawer in my night stand and he would talk to me through his letters. I held onto significant phrases, reminders of what was most important to my husband and insight to what is still important to him. Each night he seemed to say exactly what I needed to hear and he answered questions I had in my heart.

My Dear Sweet Wife,　　　　　*10 Jan '91*

How do you like this stationary! It is compliments of the American Legion in Kansas. Right before we left, some old veterans were giving out care packages with all kinds of hooah stuff in it.

Well Sweetheart we are in a compound right by the city of Riyadh. This place is an open target for a Terrorist attack. I've got my guys going everywhere two by two for security reasons. Our accommodations are not too bad we've got running water and electricity although we can only take showers every three days! (Right up my alley huh!)

Hey sweetie how are you doing? I wrote Dale and petitioned (pleaded) with him to stay with you, so that I can have a little peace of mind. I hope your drive went well and that all of the boxes and stuff gets to you okay! Please let me know as soon as possible about work (phone #) school, getting stickers for Davis Monthan AFB, and getting your hospital card! Just let me know what's going on so I don't worry.

I'm doing a lot better now though I still miss you more than I can stand it. I keep telling myself that this is the last time I'm going to do this to you or me. I love you so very much and I can't wait to get our family started. Take Care Sweetheart,

I Love You Eternally

Joey

Joe always delivered my answers. It was a clear message to me. The children and I were still his number one concern and priority. I knew he would continue to visit us and watch over us. I still had hope for a special dream or vision of him but for now I was comforted by the messages I already had.

This was the second letter he had signed "Joey." I don't remember thinking too much about it when I received the letters, even though he had never referred to himself as Joey. But now, as I was picking apart and analyzing every letter, I wondered if this was a sign of him feeling vulnerable as he faced going into battle. I felt like I was getting to know my husband more now as I was more capable of feeling what he had felt.

I wrote about this subject in my journal:

Tonight I watched a show that was about a holocaust survivor. She told one man that some people couldn't handle her story; she said that "their heart couldn't feel and their mind couldn't conceive the pain." It almost feels like a club I've joined, Joe, the compassionate club. Some people really listen to my story and I can feel their sorrow for me but others just can't come close to feeling for me. I'm almost attracted to those who have lost a loved one or experienced great heartache. Then I know we can truly relate and we can feel the depth of each others pain. Sometimes I can just see an empty stair from some people (kinda' like I used to have) and I just don't even have the desire to talk to them.

I used to be the one with the empty stare as Joe tried to share his feelings with me while he struggled through both joining the church and getting married against his parents' wishes and as he shared his experiences in the Gulf War. I could only have a desire to feel what he was feeling back then. Now I sit and think of all the difficult situations he was in and I weep for him and my heart feels his pain to a depth it couldn't before. Now my "heart can feel" and my "mind can conceive the pain."

CHAPTER 11

"Children are an Heritage of the Lord"
Psalms 127:3

Joe and I had discussed starting our family while he was in Ranger School but I didn't feel ready for motherhood at the time. It overwhelmed me to think about the time and energy it takes to care for a child. I watched my sisters as their little ones protested bedtime and made messes and needed, needed, needed! But Joe going to war changed all those feelings of inadequacy into a strong desire to start our family—just like many other women in the history of soldiers coming home from war!

A month after Joe got home we found out I was pregnant and Joe gave me a high five. "Good job, Babes!" Like I had won a race or something!

We had one week of anticipating having our baby

and announcing it to everyone. We didn't anticipate having a miscarriage. I was so sad and worried that I wouldn't be able to have children. But as I shared what had happened with other women they assured me of how common it was to have a miscarriage with the first pregnancy. We also remembered the blessing Joe had given me which included a promise of us having children, so we didn't lose all hope.

My first semester at Kansas State University and a couple little jobs kept me busy. We moved from our Junction City apartment into on-Post housing (a two-story duplex). Ft. Riley, Kansas is a beautiful area with rolling hills of green grass and trees. Buildings on "main post," (where the highest ranking officers lived) date back to Custer. Museums, monuments and historical homes dot the area. I loved to play the soundtrack from the movie *Glory* while riding around Post. With this dramatic music accompanying me, I couldn't help but have some dramatic scene in my head. Besides the scenes from the movie, *Glory*, I created a slide show of Joe in action, with his various uniforms as a cadet and an officer. This music became his theme song in my mind. It was also great background music when family came to visit for the first time. Everyone who visited us from out of town would get the *Glory* tour. I was proud to show off where we lived.

That December we flew to Florida to spend

Christmas with Joe's family. During the flight I began to feel extremely sick. I had just taken a pregnancy test a week before, and it was negative so I didn't think it was morning sickness. The nauseous feeling did not go away as we landed and drove to their home. Mamie was preparing some serious soul food for dinner that night. It wasn't the best time to be introduced to the smell of soaking chit'lins! A couple days into our stay I took another pregnancy test and it confirmed what I had hoped. We were pregnant!

His mother and sisters weren't as happy as I had hoped they'd be, "It might not be accurate. You should wait till you go to the doctor." I knew my mother-in-law wanted me to finish my degree before I got pregnant—I still had another year and a half to go. Waiting a year to get pregnant was the logical thing to do, but I don't always do the logical thing. I was upset that she wasn't happy about it. Joe was happy though. He had that same strong desire to start our little family and not wait.

I finished my second semester as my abdomen gradually grew to the size of a basketball. I lost weight everywhere else. It seemed that everything I ate went directly to the womb to nourish this little baby, so there was none left for me. My sister, Danette, was with me when the doctor "prescribed" daily cheesecake and milk shakes made with thick cream—as many as I could handle. She was jealous but bought me a Dairy Queen blizzard on our way home, with a reminder, "Doctors orders!"

At about six months I started going into premature labor. The doctor put me on bed rest and prescribed terbutaline to calm the contractions. It sure didn't calm my nerves though. It made my heart race and my hands shake. We learned I couldn't be trusted with breakables after a few plates ended up on the floor.

Joe stressed over doing the grocery shopping. He got me a map of the commissary with a list of the foods in each aisle so I could write my shopping list in the order of where the product was. (Yes, we struggled before cell phones!) If I put "sliced cheese," he would complain that I wasn't specific enough. "There were a lot of different sliced cheeses", he said, and how was he supposed to know which one? He had no problem, however, picking out the right kind of powdered doughnuts and Pop Tarts, and they weren't even on the list! Soon after I was put on bed rest Joe gave me the sweetest gift—a stool for the kitchen so I could continue to cook! Joe had a lot of talents, but cooking wasn't one he liked to work on. One time when he visited a major at his home he was surprised that this man asked him to wait while he got his brownies out of the oven. Joe was amazed that a major in the Army was baking! This concept was so foreign to him.

Close to the end of my eighth month I had an unusually long wait for the doctor at one of my regular checks because someone was having quadruplets! Sitting in a hard chair for too long made me go into labor. I thought they were only Braxton Hicks but the doctor confirmed that they were contractions and I was dilating. I was admitted to the hospital which was upstairs from where my check up was. Joe was called from work as I was given high doses of terbutaline to stop labor. Joe was there to witness an amniocentesis to test the baby's lungs, and a steroid shot to strengthen them. Needles were coming at me from every direction. After I had the amniocentesis, which was so extremely painful that I held onto the bed posts behind me, Joe said he would have a chat with this child if he or she ever gave me grief! When contractions continued, I was sent by ambulance to Topeka! Joe and I were both nervous as they loaded me in. He had to drive behind, not knowing what would happen next. When I arrived at the Topeka Hospital I was given an IV of magnesium sulfate, enough to slowly take away all reflexes. I felt like my whole body had been numbed at the dentist. Joe tried not to laugh too much as my speech became slurred but at least the contractions stopped. Even though this was traumatic, I was kind of happy to be there. I had a few nurses checking on me, rubbing my leg as they asked, "How you doin' sweetie?" The décor was lovely also, very cozy and calming. Military hospitals don't quite have the same feel!

The next day a doctor informed me that I was stable enough to be sent back to the hospital on Post. I was able to go home that next day after they determined I was stable. I only needed to keep my baby in for another week, so I was advised to stop taking the terbutaline the next Friday night.

There was no doubt the terbutaline was keeping me from going into labor because the contractions started early Saturday morning. We went straight to the hospital and a nurse looked at me and laughed as she said, "Girl, you're still smiling. You're not havin' that baby for awhile! Why don't you go on a walk and come back later!"

We went to the mall to buy baby furniture, stopping periodically for a contraction to pass. After the shopping trip, Joe took me home and then left to pick up my brother, Dale and his new wife, Sharron, who had planned this visit a while back. Joe had to drive two hours away to the Kansas City airport. I stayed home and went through labor without knowing what stage I was in or what kind of pain I should or shouldn't be feeling or how close I was to having a baby. When Joe finally showed up I couldn't even get up off the couch to greet our guests. I half smiled and quietly said, "Welcome to Kansas." I told Joe that the hospital would have to admit me because I couldn't take much more of this intense pain! He called the hospital and a nurse had him time my contractions.

After he told her how close my contractions were, she quickly responded, "Get her here immediately!" We left Dale and Sharron at the house and rushed to the hospital as I had contraction after contraction. Just 45 minutes after entering the hospital, I delivered a healthy baby.

Our titles changed that night. "It's a boy!" the doctor announced. Joe instantly looked like a dad, and I instantly felt like a mom: tired, overwhelmed, and filled with emotions—mostly joy. Tears flowed as I held our baby boy.

Joe's journal:

Joseph Oliver Reed IV came into this world at 2215, 18 July 1992, 5lbs, 11.3 oz, 18 ½ inches long, Irwin Army Community Hospital, Ft. Riley, Kansas.

We brought Joey home on Monday, 20 July 1992. I still can't believe he is ours forever. His first night home he cried all night long and Darla and I got no sleep at all. His second night was a lot better but we were so tired from the first night that we hardly noticed the difference.

Before we all turned in we held our first family prayer with Joey. What a spiritual experience to pray on behalf of your family, thanking Heavenly Father for the blessings of life. Darla cried a bit for realizing that our dreams were coming true.

Joey has gotten better throughout this first week. Changing his diaper is still a 4 hand job however Darla and I have gotten it down to a two person battle drill.

This little child occupied every moment of my day. I didn't try to do anything else. Feed, sleep, change, bathe, and admire this absolutely perfect baby was about all I could do. Joe would come home to a disaster area with the baby and me asleep in the middle of it. I did have continuous visitors who helped those first few weeks. After Dale and Sharron left, my parents, and my two youngest siblings, Doug and Diana came. The next week, Mamie and Daria showed up and were amazed with how much this tiny baby looked just like his dad.

Since we had four Joe's in the family now and the nick names Joey, Junior, and Little Joe had already been taken, I wanted to call him J.R. Joe didn't totally agree until he heard his mother calling him by this name. We also established names for the grandparents. My parents were fine with Grandma and Grandpa. They had already welcomed these titles long before J.R. came along. But Joe's parents felt much too young and needed to ease into this new stage of life. They decided on "Mamie" and "Pop."

When J.R. was a few months old, I took him to Florida to see Mamie, Pop, and his Auntie Daria. Mamie and I got our days confused and I was there one day before they were expecting us. She took advantage of the mix up to surprise Pop. When he drove up, we put J.R. in his car seat and set him on the floor so right when Pop walked in, he would be greeted by his grandson. We hid and watched as Pop stopped in his tracks, looked at this baby, looked around, and then looked at the baby again. The confused look on his face was priceless. He later shared that he was saying to himself, "This kid looks familiar!" It was so fun to watch them dote over their grandson, and I got to know them a little better and felt more comfortable around them.

Joe's journal:

4 Jan. '93

As I reflect on the past two months I

can see how we have been greatly blessed by the Lord's hand. As we traveled to Arizona for thanksgiving we ran into a blizzard while going through the northern pan handle of Texas. It was JR's first long car ride and he was doing quite well, he slept almost all the way. The blizzard got really bad around Shamrock, Texas at the eastern border of the Texas pan handle. As I continued to push west trying to get to Amarillo, TX, the first exit to the town of Groom, TX, we ran into some cars and trucks stopped in the middle of the road. The ice on the road was at least 2 inches thick and visibility was barely 3 feet in front of the car. I had slammed on the brakes and spun the car around so I wouldn't hit the vehicles stopped in the road. (I was only going 30 mph) We ended up with our front end stuck in the median and it was useless trying to back out. It was only 1130 and already the skies were dark, we were low on gas and knew we could not run the car for heat for very long. After about an hour, Darla and I realized the gravity of our predicament and decided that it was time to ask for the Lord's help. We offered our humble prayer and in less than 30 minutes on the east bound side of the highway a man stopped his truck and walked across the highway toward us. I rolled down my window to speak with him and he beckoned us to wrap up the baby and he would take us to a warm, safe place in Groom. We did as he instructed and in 10 minutes found ourselves in a Methodist church with many, many other stranded people. After thanking him he returned to the dangerous roads to rescue other travelers. The first answer to prayer.

Later in the day my concern over abandoning our car was growing. All of our belongings were in it as well as it being our mode of transportation. Again I offered a prayer but this one was silent. Knowing that the only way to get my car back was to go do something, I went out into the blizzard and waved down a wrecker. The driver informed me that I would have to wait because there were so many cars on the highway. He pointed to another truck to take me back to the church. I noticed that the man driving the truck had a bungee cord to pull cars out from being *stuck. I asked him to please pull me out because I had a hitch to which we could pull the car out with. He conceded, and we spent an hour looking up and down the highway for my snow ridden car. We finally found it, pulled it out and returned to the church. I paid him for his services and counted my blessings.*

The next day we finally got back on the road headed toward Lubbock. Although travel was slow we arrived with a decision to make, whether to go south to Lubbock, Texas or west to Albuquerque, New Mexico. Again we offered a prayer and decided to head south. About 30 miles out of Lubbock the roads cleared, the sun was shining and we resumed normal highway travel. Again prayer was answered. We arrived in Willcox early Thanksgiving morning safe and sound.

Joe was called to be the elder's quorum president, which meant he was in charge of a majority of the men in our ward and their families. He would have meetings with his counselors and secretary in our home and since our home was so small, I couldn't help but hear some of the dialogue. All of them were in the military so it didn't sound like your average elder's quorum presidency meeting: "Roger that," "Hooah," "Say again over?" "That's a big no-go," "Affirmative," "Roger dodger." Acronyms and army verbiage were intertwined with the important discussion of caring for those who were in need. One family I remember him helping consisted of a single mother with three children. Gail was struggling with her oldest boy and he wasn't doing well in school. Joe made a homework chart for him and talked to him about making goals and how important good grades were. Gail said Joe Reed was like "E.F. Hutton" in her home; when he spoke, everyone listened! He visited them on a regular basis.

I think of Gail often as I struggle alone with my three children. I remember a conversation we had when she expressed her feelings of inadequacy as a mother. She cried as she worried about how well she was doing. I assured her everything would be okay. I felt for her but I couldn't relate like I can now. Oh how I can now relate with the overwhelming feeling behind those tears!

One of Joe's elder's quorum counselors, Tim Thomas, wrote the following letter to the children after Joe died.

I met your father right after Desert Storm in August 1991 in Junction City,

Kansas. We met at The Church of Jesus Christ of Latter Day Saints. My knowledge of your father really started while I served as one of his counselors. During our first meeting, he described what he wanted to accomplish as a presidency. This was typical of your father; he always had a goal in mind or knew what needed to be accomplished. During subsequent meetings I felt and knew he loved his wife, your mother. She truly was his sweetheart. It was through her that he had learned about the Church and he loved the gospel of Jesus Christ. The strength of his testimony was so firm and solid, and I have never heard one so touching or more inspiring than the one of your father's.

Acts of kindness and concern for others were two of the many characteristics of your father. Let me share a story about love and the Good Samaritan. The status of Leslie W. today is not known to me, however, I can truly tell you, your father showed compassion and love for this man on several occasions.

Leslie had been a soldier in the Army, not just any old soldier but an infantryman, like your father at the time. Life for Leslie was hard, because he had not been able to find regular work and was struggling to have the essentials of life. Leslie lived in a three room apartment in the center of town; windows that were broken and some missing panes, doors that did not fit the frames due to the age of the building, and floors that creaked almost with every step. Due to the hardships, Leslie could not afford electricity to light the apartment at night, or gas to heat it either. Leslie had no car and mostly walked wherever he needed to go.

The season was late fall and the Kansas winter was almost upon us. During one of our presidency meetings, Joe asked if we could go down and help this brother. On a cold Saturday morning, Joe, Myron, and I, went over to Leslie's apartment to install clear plastic and weather stripping over the windows. This was my first visit to Leslie's apartment and I was astonished to find anyone living this primitively. As we worked to perform this service, I *listened to Brother W. express his deep appreciation for the work we were doing. He described how cold it was getting at night and without heat or light he would often go for long walks. The long walks would tire him and help him to sleep throughout the night. After the work was completed, Leslie was the first to notice how much warmer the apartment felt because the plastic and weather stripping was blocking the windy drafts. As we departed Brother W.'s apartment, Joe expressed his gratitude to us for the service we had rendered. I left the apartment with the knowledge and assurance I truly had done some good that day.*

Joe's service did not stop there. Leslie slept on an old Army cot and not a real bed. Sleeping on a cot is better than sleeping on the ground some might say, especially if you are an infantryman. Through Joe's effort a real bed was obtained and given to Leslie. The candles that use to light the night for Leslie were replaced by lanterns. The cold was replaced by heat from a space heater. All of these things helped the physical life of Leslie W.

I remember an occasion, which your mother could tell you about more clearly than I, but I know of it through the words of Leslie. During the Thanksgiving season families get together and celebrate those things we are thankful for and set down to large feast of turkey and ham, dressing and gravy, pies and cakes, and etc. Mostly men and occasionally women set down to watch the football games and parades on television. For Leslie none of this would have been possible, if it had not been for the kindness and generosity of your parents. Your father, probably having discussed it with your mother first, extended an invitation to Leslie to share Thanksgiving Day with them. I remember how Leslie bragged about how much he thoroughly enjoyed his time with your family that day.

Just like the Good Samaritan in the Bible, your father not only saw to the needs of a stranger but took care of him like a brother. Prior to Joe's departure from Junction City and Fort Riley, he came to me and gave me the charge to look after Leslie and I did my best until my departure. When I left Fort Riley,

Leslie had moved into a trailer. He was able to work and afford the essentials, like electricity. He was starting to have a few luxury items also, like a television. Your father saw Leslie through some difficult times and I feel confident in saying, somewhere in the eternity's, Leslie will bear testimony that your father rendered a service and showed love for him like no other, except the Savior himself.

A woman in our ward in Kansas paid Joe a great compliment. It was after he had shared his feelings about the Lord and the church at an activity. She told me that there are many men who are beautiful on the outside alone, and there are many men who are beautiful on the inside alone, but Joe was one of the few who was beautiful inside and out! I had to agree.

A few years later, as I spoke to my therapist about my next to perfect husband, he said that many people idealized their loved ones after they die. He didn't understand. I bragged about Joe like this while he was alive. Yes, he had his faults. I didn't think he complimented me enough on a daily basis. I was blessed to have all the compliments in letters, but in person he didn't like being too mushy. He was a perfectionist about a clean house. Most of the time, I was too tired to pick up at night before going to bed but he would throw out the scenario of a fire or another emergency happening in the middle of the night and we'd trip over the toys and not get out of the house in time. Keeping track of finances was also something he took to a level I didn't think was necessary. I hated trying to remember how I had spent that $20 cash so he could do a pie chart, "Um, a happy meal for the kids….um …postage stamps…." But when I was annoyed with him, I would think of all the characteristics he had that I loved and they always out-weighed the things I didn't like.

Now, I wish I had someone to do a financial pie chart for me and someone besides me who cared about the state of our home. Now that I am responsible for everything, I think back and wish I could have a do-over. If I could have Joe back, I would keep track of my expenses for him and I'd be grateful he was helping me pick up the house at night. I'd be less dependent on him and his time home. As a company commander, he left at 5:00 AM and didn't get home until 7:30 or 8:00 PM, and I complained. If I had him back I'd be grateful he was there to help get the kids to bed and I'd be happy to have my once a week date night with him. With my new perspective, I regret being so carefree and letting him worry about the mortgage and life insurance, taxes and bills. Now

I was forced to take on all the worries of the household. Now I was forced to feel the stress he had felt.

The year anniversary of his death came and went. In May, Memorial Day weekend, I attended a seminar in Washington DC for widows and other family members of military who have died. The organization is called Tragedy Assistance Program for Survivors (TAPS). It helped my attitude to be able to meet other military widows. I wasn't the only one who was dealing with such a traumatic loss. My friend, Diane, who persuaded me to go, was not only dealing with her husband's death, but also her son's – both were military related. I'm grateful for her friendship and the time we had at the TAPS seminar to talk. She was strong and a great example to me. She was able to take the harshness of life and accept it as a test. She didn't ask, "Why?" She asked, "What should I do now and what am I supposed to learn from this?" When the founder of TAPS first called me to tell me how glad she was that I was coming and that we were going to have so much fun, I was thinking, "No, I haven't been in the mood to have fun for over a year now, thank you." But it proved to be kind of fun to connect with so many other widows and find things to laugh about. One time Diane and I were on the escalators to go upstairs to a meeting but instead of continuing up on the next set of escalators we got on the one that brought us right back to where we started. We joked that the widow following the widow was worse than the blind following the blind.

Back at home, I was blessed to have another really good friend whom I met through my mother-in-law. Agnes was a widow also, and we became close friends quickly as we could relate to each other so well. Her husband had passed away just a couple months after Joe, so we were at about the same stage of grieving. We could relate with the loneliness that came with the loss of a spouse, as well as the changed social life. But as lonely as we both felt, we agreed that our husbands set the standard and we were not lonely enough to lower the bar. We really enjoyed our dinners out and other social events together. We liked to be catered to and Agnes taught me that it was okay to choose the optimal spot in a restaurant in order to enhance our dining experience. Our surroundings really affected our spirits so if we could be by the beautiful mural or by the fireplace, we would! Diane and Agnes were so crucial in helping me to feel like I was not alone.

One night after getting the babies to bed I stayed up late, watching TV. There were some interesting movies coming on; one about slavery and one about the integration of schools. In the one about slavery, a baby was torn from her mother's arms to be sold, and a father was killed in front of his young son. Even though the slave owner forbade his slaves to learn to read, a young slave girl had the desire to learn and so an elderly man taught her late at night when no one would know. When they were discovered, the "master" cut off one of the elderly man's fingers. This man picked his finger up and wrote his name in the dirt with it, saying the letters as he wrote them and then saying his name as he looked at his young student with conviction. As I watched this movie I sobbed for all of them. Their hardships seemed unbearable! I also felt a great admiration for their strength and I felt ashamed for thinking I had it so bad. That night I told myself to shut up and stop complaining! My life seemed so easy compared to theirs, my trials like a walk in the park.

My attitude changed a bit after that night. I began to look around me and notice others who have their own burden to carry. And I began to realize that there were quite a few people I would not want to trade trials with!

My journal:

September 1997

People say, "Time heals all wounds." Well, I have found that to be untrue, because I know this "wound" will never "heal." But what has changed is that I have started to accept this wound, to accept this pain as a part of my life. A majority of the people of this world who have ever lived are dealing with their own pain. Who am I to not have to struggle? Time has taken me through the numbness, the anger, the sadness, and the acceptance, but the pain will always remain. There will always be a yearning in my heart to be with my love, to be in his arms again and time will never change that.

My intense inside-out cries happened less frequently. Besides my attitude change, I learned to protect myself a little more. A huge part of widowhood is the drastic change in social life. No more military balls, no more Hale and Farewells, no more being taken out, no more planned dates with other couples. The social events I attended would sometimes leave me with a huge reminder of what I didn't have anymore. If there were too many couples or too many situations where I was left feeling alone and awkward, or even if it took too much energy to get myself to the event, I would come home and need to have a good cry. Movies were another issue. I didn't watch Titanic for many years because I was afraid my heart couldn't handle it, the song alone was enough to get me going.

The question of whether or not there could ever be anyone else in my life would seep into my mind occasionally. It was always on everyone else's minds. Without fail, everyone I talked to would eventually ask. I didn't like trying to explain. It wasn't a simple yes or no answer. I let God know that I would not be putting any effort toward finding another man because I only had enough time and energy for my children. It would be like finding a missing puzzle piece with a peculiar shape in order to fit. This seemed way too complicated, so I handed the task over to Him. I also made it clear that if there was someone who could fit into my life, I needed him to be right in front of me because I had things to do. So I placed an order with God and said, "If it is meant to be, it will happen."

This man God found would have to be beautiful inside and out, just like Joe. It'd be better if he was a widower, who was married in the temple, and loved his wife with all his heart. Who else could handle the idea that after having a relationship with him in this life, I looked forward to being with Joe in the next? He would also have to love the Lord and His church. After placing this order, I still worried. If and when the Lord found this man, if my order stood in front of me, with all the criteria, was I capable of falling in love? Joe filled so much of my heart. Was there room for anyone else?

CHAPTER 12

Keep On Movin'

Joe's journal:

23 Jan. 1993

> *...Our son Joseph is growing and developing constantly. He learns and displays new characteristics every day. I love him so! I hope I can be the kind of Dad he deserves!*

Just before J.R.'s first birthday, we were on the road to our next area. We always went the long way around: to travel from Ft. Riley, Kansas, to Ft. Benning, Georgia, we went through New York, down to Florida, and then on to our destination. Joe was anxious to go back to West Point and get pictures with his son. We also had to visit his friends Kevin and Michele Doman. Joe and Kevin had had many deep conversations about God and their goals for the future as well as talks about me as he impatiently waited for me to finish my mission. It was so good to see them. In Jersey, Joe's sister, Vonda, had J.R.'s birthday party planned. Aunts, uncles, grandparents, cousins, and even J.R.'s great great grandmother was there. There aren't too many people who have a picture with their great great grandmother and Joe didn't want to let that chance slip by. J.R. wasn't feeling well that day, but we got the picture!

At the end of our stay at Ft. Riley, Joe had taken tests and petitioned to change from Infantry to Aviation. We traveled through Washington, DC, so that he could personally visit the office of those who made the decision of letting him into flight school. He not only wanted to thank them personally but to help them get to know him so that when his name appeared in their paperwork, they would have a face associated with the name. We then stopped in South Carolina to visit his other grandparents (Big Mama and Granddaddy – his mom's parents) and then on to Orlando to visit his parents.

Back at Ft. Benning, Georgia, Joe attended the Infantry Officer Advanced Course, before transferring from Infantry to Aviation. We were only there for six months. This time we had a nicer apartment with a playground for J.R. We were back in the same ward, where Joe was called to be the young men president.

Joe's journal:

2 January 1994

I can't believe a whole year has passed since my last entry into this journal. So many wonderful things have occurred this past year that I will only be able to recount a few significant events. The most recent event was this past Christmas at Mom and Dad's in Orlando. The whole family was together under one roof. Our lives are so richly blessed. J.R. has developed a special relationship with his grandfather; he calls him "Pop." Vonda is just about done with her Masters Degree in Corporate and Public Communications from Seton Hall. Daria has finished her first semester of College at Columbia College in Missouri. I hope she soon buckles down and gets serious about her future. Mom is still the thread that knits our family together; her love and devotion is always something to look forward to when coming home. What was most significant about our trip was that Pop-pop flew down from New Jersey to attend Daria's Debutante Ball. Nanny was counseled to rest at home by her Doctor so she didn't make the trip. But under one roof we had four generations of Joseph O. Reed. I felt the spirit of Elijah as Dad expressed his appreciation for his family during an evening meal. I gained a deeper understanding of what is written in the chapter of Malachi, "as the hearts of the children turn to the fathers and the hearts of the fathers to the children."

Another significant event occurred yesterday as we watched television in our little apartment. Darla and I were not really paying attention to what J.R. was doing until he turned off the television. Naturally our first reaction was to tell him to turn it back on, but before we could say anything J.R. folded his arms and bowed his head and said, "pay" (pray.) He wanted to offer prayer with the family. We had not yet offered thanks to our Heavenly Father for our safe and enjoyable trip, so we entreated J.R.'s request and knelt and prayed. I *am amazed at how much he learns by watching us. We had not formally taught him to turn off the TV and pray but he learned through our example that when we converse with Deity all of our attention should be there focused. The power of example is the greatest. I will always remember the day an 18 month old child reminded his father, an elder in Israel, to offer thanksgiving to God after returning safely home from a long trip.*

Ft. Rucker, Alabama was our next stop, where Joe attended flight school. We rented a house in Enterprise and Joe was again called to be young men president. I began to think about having another child. I felt like a little girl was ready to come; it was like she was trying to say, "It's my turn now!" I didn't profess to have a revelation at the time. I wasn't sure if it was just me coming up with these ideas on my own or not, but my feelings were strong enough that we decided it was time. It didn't take long before I was showing Joe the positive sign on the pregnancy test. Five months into my pregnancy I was admitted into the hospital for premature labor. I sat and cried at the thought of being on bed rest again. But with all the tests they took, they were able to tell me what gender the baby was. I left the hospital smiling, knowing that we were indeed going to have a little girl. Throughout my pregnancy I kept having these thoughts of an anxious little girl ready to come. Now that I know my Jasmine, I'm absolutely positive the feelings I had were real! I don't doubt she was trying to talk to me long before she came.

Jasmine was born sooner than we had anticipated. I was going to go off my medication on a Friday because it would have been easier on Joe if she came on the weekend. Her early arrival was my fault. Instead of following the doctor's orders to stay off my feet, that Monday I tried to do some Christmas shopping. I leaned on my cart and walked slowly, thinking that would keep me safe! But it didn't. The contractions started the next day. Again, I went through most of the labor at home as I waited for Joe. But this time I had J.R. keeping me company. He would climb on my back when I was on my knees, leaning over the couch in pain. Joe got home just in time to rush J.R. to some friends and me to the hospital. I was only at the hospital for 30 minutes before Jasmine came shooting out! "Welcome to the world, my little anxious one!"

She was our favorite Christmas present under the tree that year. It was the first Christmas morning we had alone as a family. Joe and I read, "The Christmas Box" together the night before, which helped bring the spirit of Christmas into our home. It was such a peaceful feeling. It affected us so much that we resolved to read it every year. J.R. was now old enough to know about Santa and Jesus, which made the morning even more fun. Our newborn slept through the unwrapping of gifts, which we thought was a miracle. The Mormon Tabernacle Choir serenaded us with Christmas music throughout the morning and after the presents were all unwrapped I sat feeding our baby while Joe and J.R. played with their new toys. It is a memory I will always cherish.

Joe's journal:

21 December 1994

Well enough days have past that I should have 4 of these journals finished. Nonetheless I will repent and do better in the future.

Since we moved here to Alabama for flight school life has been good to us. Besides the fact that Mom and Dad visited us from Florida, we have been blessed with another sweet child in our home. Jasmine Alexandria Reed came sprinting into the world at 7:04 PM on 13 December 1994 weighting in at 6 pounds and 19 ½ inches long.

She is a beautiful baby just like J.R. was when he was born. Darla is such a champ. She seems to recoil and recover from having these children so easily. My cup truly overfloweth in the blessings of having a celestial companion and two sweet children that enrich my life so abundantly. So far Jasmine has proven to be a much more manageable baby than was J.R. She sleeps constantly and only cries to eat, burp or wants a diaper change.

Flight school has been a fairly good challenge. I am coming to a close in my flight school training though. Two more days of advanced combat skills, then four weeks of nights. It looks as though I will get an advanced aircraft transition to the OH-58D Kiowa Warrior. I am definitely looking forward to flying that aircraft.

Joe studied hard to learn how to fly the Apache. I quizzed him every night on every procedure necessary to fly and land safely. He graduated and we were off to our next area—Ft. Bragg, North Carolina, where we were looking forward to a longer stay of three to four years.

After our extensive road trip across the country and back we were ready to settle into our new home. We learned what most new home owners learn, that the home is usually not ready on the estimated date. We stayed in temporary housing on Post for a couple months while we waited for our first purchased home to be finished. It was just like a hotel room with a community kitchen down stairs if we wanted to cook. It was free and we had our new home to look forward to. Picking out all the details was so exciting: yellow siding, green door, white linoleum with black diamonds, speckled Formica, white walls (because our last home we rented had dark wooden panels with small windows and I needed the exact opposite). It was really our house. I can picture the moment we first sat at our table in our new home after being in between homes for almost two months. Joe put on one of our favorite CDs with a variety of spiritual songs and he chose the song with applicable words: "There's a place for every soul that's lost, there is a way back home, no matter where you roam…" We sat and smiled at each other, so happy to be in our own home.

Another significant event happened at that time. Joe's mom and sisters were in town after the family reunion in Jersey (right after our house was done) and we were eating out for dinner. Joe's mom asked if he had any eligible men in mind for his sister. He mentioned Damon, a friend from West Point, who was now stationed at Ft. Bragg. With Mamie's encouragement, Joe invited him to join us. It would take a few years but Damon and Vonda did get married, and of course they knew they had Joe's blessing.

I gave Joe such a party that year; it was his thirtieth. There were quite a few West Point grads stationed at Ft. Bragg so I invited them all. I told the wives to wrap their husbands' most prized possession and we would pretend to give it to Joe as a birthday present. I kept the party a secret from Joe until right before. I had to let him in on the gifts he would be opening so he would play along. One of the gifts was a collection of intricate fly fishing lures. As Joe reacted with excitement and shared his plans to take J.R. fishing, the guy who owned this most prized collection turned bright red and looked like he was getting sick. Each of the men in the room was shocked as their own precious memento was unwrapped. Joe played it up and commented on how he would cherish his gifts and play with them with his children, especially the perfect replicas of the West Point cannons, which were most likely pricey and definitely not to be played with. The wives played along too, smiling back at their spouses and ignoring their questioning eyes. The room was filled with laughter and sighs of relief when they learned it was all a prank. I will never forget the sincere "thank you" Joe gave me for throwing that party for him. I'm so grateful I did.

Joe had acquired some new titles in just a few short months: captain, company commander, and second counselor in the ward bishopric. I was proud to be his wife, so unaware of how our three-to-four year plan at Ft. Bragg would be drastically cut short in less than two months after his thirtieth birthday celebration and that seven months after his birthday I'd be living by his parents, being forced to learn my way around the Orlando area.

One night, after moving into our Florida home, after a long day of dressing, feeding, changing, and cleaning up after my three little demanding children, I sat in bed, thinking about the changes in my life and needing some kind of message from their daddy. The letter I pulled out made me chuckle a little, "Yes Joe, I'm slowly realizing that this is not just another week in the field." I spoke back to him as his comments related to my situation now. All his letters had a message for me, but there was something about his letters from the war that gave me a feeling of really communicating with my husband. Sometimes I wondered if he wanted to talk to me as much as I wanted him to. This letter seemed like a reassuring, "Yes."

My Dearest Darlita,   12 Jan 1991

How are you doing? I hope that by now you have settled down and realized that this is not going to be just another week in the field. For the first few days I thought that I was in a dream/nightmare! Nothing seemed real and I just wanted to wake up. Last night my platoon and I were assigned roving guard for about a block of the military compound here. Understand that this compound has thousands of troops waiting for their equipment to get in off the ships, so this mission has some responsibility assigned to it. Right now I'm sitting down listening for all of my guard post to give situation report over the walkie-talkie. Nothing serious has happened yet though we've had to check out a few occurrences with some of the workers in the area. Things like this mission are helping me to get a better grip on what's going on and accept the fact that I'm over here and I need to deal with it the best way I can.

I wish I could call you like I could in the Mountains of Ranger School, I really want to hear your sweet voice. I hope that I can find some privacy within the next few days to make a tape for you. It seems as though I always have something to tell you or to share with you but I can't get it all out on paper. There always seems to be something that I leave out or forget to write down. Well guess who I spoke to yesterday? Yep my sweetheart! I'm so glad I found out about those phones. Speaking to you is like communing with the angels, it was heavenly.

Well since I'm going to call you in the morning I'm gonna cut this letter short, although I need you to go to Radio Shack and buy me another microphone for my recorder. I think I have misplaced (lost) it somewhere so I need another ASAP. K?

Take care Babes!

Yours For Eternity,

Joe

CHAPTER 13

"A Time to Laugh"
Ecclesiastes 3:4

My journal:

March 22, 1998

I used to just stress over what to wear and what to fix for dinner, having children brought on a few more challenges, and responsibilities. How I wish I could go back to that life, when my husband was helping. Now I have property taxes and escrows to figure out, income tax to file, car maintenance, yard work, medical insurance, investments, home maintenance, decorating, gardening, fixing meals, feeding (spoon feeding most of the time) three children, "I wanna hug you", "I'm hungry", "I want juice", "play with me", "just a minute honey, I'm writing out bills", "one more phone call", "$12.00 left in my checking account?", "2 more phone calls", "I'm cooking now", "right after I do the dishes", take out the garbage, vacuum, kiss a boo boo, fix a bike, put up shelves, clean the garage, "eggie san'wich" for 3, send off pictures to Nanny, get more salt in the water filter, help with homework, -play dough? Exercise, shampoo rug, change that diaper, change the oil, more gas for the mower, oh, you have to put oil in the mower too? Clean the a/c filter, water the plants, read scriptures, Jessica's covered in soup, J.R. is sick, Jasmine confused food for finger paint, the grass is turning yellow, more fertilizer, spray the bugs, smash the spider, volunteer at the school, church calling... what do I want to do for a career? Maybe I will have time to think about that next year! I know it will get easier, I'm going to slap the next woman who says, "It doesn't get easier it just gets different." Don't bust my bubble, I have to have *that hope that as my children get older, they will help me, and home and yard and child maintenance will be a little easier. If it doesn't get easier I will most definitely have a nervous break down. And how was your day Joe?*

I'm sure his days in heaven weren't classified as hectic but this letter reminded me of one hectic day he did have.

My Dearestest Darla,   Friday 18 Jan 91
                        10:35 AM

I'm sorry that I could not call you this morning however I'm sure you know what has happened! We were asleep when it all went down. Someone came bustin' in our room and yelled at us to get in our MOPP gear (Gas Attack Uniform) and to take our nerve agent pills. The rest of the early morning was chaotic with all kinds of rumors flying around. Anyways now we are out by the port with our vehicles awaiting transport to our assembly area out in the desert somewhere.

So were you frightened? I was for

awhile because I couldn't believe the "Real Thing" was actually going down. Last night one of Saddam's missiles headed for the city I'm in was shot down. That was pretty scary too. I didn't know I could move so fast. I don't know about you but I'm glad this mess has finally started. At least I know that we won't be stuck out here just sitting around doing nothing.

From all the news reports it sounds as though the Air Force and Navy pilots are kickin' some vicious butt in Iraq. That has morale up among the ground forces here to be used eventually. Things are going well thus far in the platoon, I've identified some weaknesses that I need to fix ASAP but otherwise things are going well.

So sweetheart how are you doing? I know you are worrying a lot about me but you are going to have to be strong. This conflict, hopefully, will end soon and we can come home to our families. Darla I am so glad that we decided to have you stay in Tucson. Despite my feelings about Tucson itself, I'm comforted with peace of mind knowing *that you have people there you can trust and take good care of you. I know I kind of disliked the idea of it for a while, but I now am pleased with the decision.*

Isn't that so typical of how the Lord works, he gives the blessing only after some faith and sacrifice has been exercised. Hey mail is going out now so take care and remember that I Love You.

Yours For All Eternity,

Joey

J.R. was so excited to go on the bus to school his first day of kindergarten. Mamie, Pop, and Vonda were all there to share his big day. The bus was significantly late but J.R. refused our offers to drive him. He wanted to ride that big yellow bus! We all cheered when it finally came and he ran to the front of the line to be the first one to board. His smile took up his whole face as he waved to us from the inside of his new ride.

The second and third day of school were no different. He was thrilled to get on the bus. So I could hardly believe it when the school called and explained that J.R. was having trouble wanting to go into his class room. The teacher, guidance counselor, and principal were all working together to coax him through the doorway. They even had to pick him up and carry him with his arms and legs stretched out and holding onto the frame of the doorway in his attempt to stop his entry. What was even less believable was that once they got him in, he stopped all resistance and acted like he was fine. He was a pleasant, well-behaved child throughout the day. They assured me that they would try to help him through this without me because they thought my presence would make things worse. By the fifth day he walked through the doorway of his classroom without any drama. At home he talked about how much he loved school but didn't have anything to say when I tried to get him to talk about this issue. I wondered if all the changes in his young life would continue to affect his behavior, though the rest of his kindergarten year was void of any more drama.

My journal:

Dearest Joseph,　　　　　*November 1997*

Today a friend commented on how well I handle my situation and how she could never survive taking care of her children without her husband. I struggle with the choice of really opening up with some friends or just letting them think that I'm some super woman. I think it helps others to think I am "super strong;" then they are somehow exempt from becoming a widow because they are too weak to handle it. Sometimes I want to say, "yeah, I'm doing fine, if fine means sobbing at least once a day, if fine means having a constant knot in my stomach; if fine means screaming at our sweet little Jessica because she won't stay off the kitchen table, if fine means demanding you to use your angel powers to keep the dang bugs out of my house, if fine means not being able to concentrate or remember anything because 98% of the time I'm either daydreaming about the past with you or how lovely it will be when I die and get to see you again, if that's fine, then yes, I'm doing just fine!

Just to clarify, sobbing for a moment is different than crying like your insides are coming out. I was able to laugh and have fun with life but there were still daily moments of remembering life with Joe and longing to have him there, laughing with me. This journal entry might sound drastic after so much time had passed and I had started to accept my reality. My journal was my therapist and that's how I was feeling in that moment, dramatic as it might sound. I guess my feelings and moods had become more intense, whether it was sadness or happiness or frustration.

I had to make a constant effort to stay calm with the children. I had to do things to help my own spirit so that I would not lose control. I bought myself flowers when grocery shopping to lift my spirits. I noticed how music affected me. I loved gospel music—my favorite CD's were by Take 6 and Whitney Houston's, "Preachers Wife" album. If I listened to the radio too much I felt more depressed and it was harder for me to control my temper. I remember losing it one time when the children were fighting over a crayon. They were all sitting around our small kitchen table with the crayon box in the center. When I could not get them to stop whining and fighting I hit the plastic box with my fist so hard that it shattered. Pieces of plastic and crayons flew everywhere! They all sat there looking at me, wide eyed and petrified. I was afraid too – afraid of what I was capable of doing with all that bottled up tension.

My Sabbath days became priceless to me. I needed to go to church and I needed spiritual music and spiritual videos all day Sunday. I needed and still need my Sabbath days to be holy. I recognized how much better I did during the week when I fed my spirit on Sunday. I also wanted to ensure that I would have any blessings God would give me from keeping this commandment. I heard that a school in California was implementing yoga for their stressed-out students. Well, I'd like to introduce all of them, and everyone else, to the idea of taking a break from the world and dedicating Sunday to God and family. This is the best de-stressing plan out there!

On the other six days of the week I worked on the physical de-stressing method. I have always enjoyed exercising, motivated by the love of a sport or by wanting to look good but now I was doing it purely for my mental health. I knew it was a way to release that tension so that I wouldn't release it on my children! I kept the tape by Steven Covey in the car, "Seven Habits of Successful Families," and listened to it over and over again. I'm still trying to get that "pause button" idea down, to be "proactive instead of reactive," and to "choose how [I'm] going to act." Attending church helped me to have the desire to be a calm, loving mom, and these tapes gave me the "how to" skills to keep it together. It helped also to have absolutely beautiful children who were ready to have fun and said incredible things to make me melt or make me laugh.

Jasmine made me laugh one moment and cry the next—sometimes I'd laugh and cry simultaneously. She usually caught me off guard. I was doing the dishes one day when she blurted out, "Why won't Daddy come back down from heaven... is he scared to jump?"

She held her hands up to the sky with her little two-year-old-arms and said, "Jump Daddy, I'll catch you, don't be afraid, come on down."

She waited with arms still stretched upward and finally said, "Why won't he jump Mommy?" I wondered if Joe was learning how to laugh and cry simultaneously too.

She really wanted to understand where heaven was... at age two and a half. "Can we fly there in an airplane? ...Let's go see Daddy, let's get on the airplane!"

When we were outside she wanted to know which way it was, she pointed in different directions and asked, "Is it over there... is it over there... is it over there?"

And then she broke my heart with, "How long does he have to stay?"

I didn't want to answer this question. "Do you

want to look at pictures of Daddy?" A frown and crossed arms let me know the answer.

"Do you want to watch Daddy on TV?"

"Yeth, Mommy, yeth!" she said with her little lisp.

She jumped up and down and clapped in approval. Her beautiful brown ringlets sticking out all over her head bounced with each jump. I put in the video of Joe when he was the president of the LDS Institute at West Point and was asked to talk about his teacher. He was so handsome in his uniform.

"I want to hug him, Mommy. Hold me up, Mommy!" She reached up to the TV, standing on tip toes, touching his image with her out-stretched hands. I picked her up and she palmed the screen the way she might have held his face if she could. She then put her face against the screen between her hands, "I hugging Daddy, Mommy."

She smiled a half smile, with the other half flattened onto the TV screen. She closed her eyes and seemed to be imagining actually being able to touch him, then she whispered, "I love you Daddy, I love you." I sobbed silently.

I decided to take my little Jasmine to the cemetery, just the two of us. We brought flowers and a helium balloon. I told her how Daddy's spirit came out of his body and floated up to heaven.

I wrote on the balloon what she wanted to say to her daddy; "Daddy, I miss you, Daddy, I love you, Daddy, I wish I could hug you."

I tried not to sob out loud. We laid down on his grave and I let the message float up to heaven.

"Daddy will catch it when it gets high enough. We can't see Daddy because he isn't in his body right now, but we'll know when he has it, when we don't see the balloon anymore."

We laid there and watched the balloon shrink until it was just a purple speck in the sky, squinting to follow it until it was no longer in sight.

"Daddy's got my balloon now! He's reading my letter!" I wondered if this was as hard for Joe as it was for me. I wonder if his spirit ached to hold his young daughter. I felt his pain as well as my own.

This seemed to satisfy Jasmine, her questions of heaven subsided. We bought lots of balloons.

Jessica and JR joined the balloon-with-a-message-to-Daddy ritual. Whenever we were at Publix grocery store I got a balloon for them and then I asked if they wanted to write on it and send it to Daddy. This is something that warmed my heart to have the privilege of knowing what was in their heart and to watch them smile as they sent their message. I think it warmed Joe's heart too. One day after getting our free balloon I asked Jessica if she wanted to send it to Daddy, she responded with, "Daddy has too many balloons up there already!"

Another day an older gentleman at the grocery store was helping us take our groceries out to the car. He complimented Jasmine on her eyes and said, "You must have your Daddy's eyes."

She quickly blurted out, "My Daddy's dead."

Her bluntness has made others very uncomfortable and they usually don't know how to respond but this man smiled and said, "Well, I'll probably see him before you do so I'll tell him hello for you." What a gentlemen.

It was Daddy's birthday again. I wanted to include the children and make it a positive celebration of their father's life. "What should we do?" I asked.

J.R.: "Bake a cake!"

Jessica jumps and claps, "A cake, a cake!"

J.R.: "But Daddy won't be able to eat it!"

Jasmine: "I know! We can bake it, and then we

can kill it, and send it to heaven!" All three laughed and clapped and jumped in approval. If anyone overheard us they would think I was morbid as I laughed hysterically at her idea.

One day Jasmine seemed to have a goal to do as many crazy things as she could. I caught her lapping up water from the cement on our back porch, "Look Mommy, I'm a doggy!" She smashed crackers all over the table, floor and herself. She submerged her hand in the yogurt, and after I got her all cleaned up, she squished the slice of American cheese through her fingers and rubbed it on her hands like lotion. I spoke out loud to Joe and told him it was his turn to clean her up.

The next day she wanted to be the baby and sit in the high chair, so I put her there and gave her oatmeal. After turning my back on her for a minute, I turned around to face the biggest mess I'd ever seen her make. Oatmeal covered every inch of her from her hair to her waist. She was smiling and finger painting on the tray.

"Jasmine!"

She jumped a little and then smiled again, "Mommy, I made a mess."

I told her she could just stay there in her mess for a while, "I want you to stay there and have a grand time… play… joy in your mess."

She rubbed her cheeks and arms, giving herself quite the spa treatment. I sat on the couch to read a book to Jessica but didn't get far before I heard Jasmine calling out, "Mommy, let me down, please! I don't want to joy in my mess anymore."

Joe must have told her what to say. Jasmine and Jessica were four and three years old, and were attending Little Fishes Preschool. I had an appointment of some kind and had to rush them a bit to be on time. So as I was finishing up my make-up, I told Jasmine to get into the van with Jessica and get buckled up in their car seats. The car was in the closed garage. When I walked out to the garage, the main door was wide open and the girls were not in the van! I sprinted to the back of the van and scanned the scene in shock at what the girls had managed to accomplish in such a short time. Jasmine and Jessica both looked up from their beach chairs and smiled at me. They had all the beach necessities spread out around them: buckets, shovels, molds to make a sand castle, Frisbees, beach balls, and the ice chest. They were stretched out with hands behind their heads, like, "Ah, this is the life!"

If I could replay this moment and do it again I would laugh and enjoy my little three and four year old, but instead I flipped out. "What are you doing?!" I started throwing everything back into the garage with all my might, yelling out a few syllables with every item I threw. "I asked you... to get... in the car!... What... were you... thinking? ...Why did you ...do this?... We... are going... to be... late!" When I finished throwing the last item back, I leaned over to face Jasmine. My face was probably red as I said with clenched teeth and tightened lips, "Why did you not get in the van like I asked you to?"

She looked at me and replied very calmly, "Mommy, after you take us to school maybe you should, you know, come back home, and watch a video, get yourself a salad, and you know, sit on the couch for a while, you know, and relax." She said it in such a concerned matter-of-fact way that I just stared at my little girl in disbelief. Was she four or thirty-four?

Staying calm continued to be my biggest challenge. I really needed my night time ritual of reading scriptures or an uplifting book and before my eyes closed for the night, a letter from my husband.

Dear Darls,   *20 January 1991*

Well sweetheart we have now moved to our assembly area out in the middle of the Arabian Desert. This place is like another planet! It is hard to believe we are still on Earth because you can't see anything but desert all around. At night we can see the flashes from the bombing raids on Iraq and Kuwait. War is so close to us now that it is becoming a regular thing with us. However none of us have really comprehended the reality of it all. Everyone speaks of what they are going to do once we return to Kansas. Compared to Saudi Arabia, Kansas is like a resort, and we all look forward to returning home.

Today is Sunday and it looks as though I'm going to have to administer the sacrament to myself because our position is far from others. Already some of my soldiers have noticed that I refrain from vulgar language and conversation. It is awkward at times because everyone seems to be engaged in some kind of lewd conversation that is naturally accompanied by similar thoughts. I don't want to seem like some kind of prima Donna, but I'm determined to maintain my standards.

Darla, I just listened to George Durrant's talk on "The Line of Scrimmage" again. Every time I listen to that tape, I am brought to the realization of how happy I am that we are married and that we were sealed in God's Holy Temple. It is a comfort to know that I have my "scholarship to be a co creator" with God and you. I am so sorry at how I acted the first few months of our marriage! I guess I was a "phony bunch of baloney" for a while there. I suppose that although I was/am overjoyed at our marriage I was also upset about disappointing my parents and putting them through so much pain. I also needed to learn how to share my things with someone else since I never had to do that in the past. Sweetheart, I guess I'm just trying to apologize for the things I've done and said, that I know have hurt you. My own foolish pride got between me and the person I love most and don't want that to happen again. Being away like this under life and death circumstances makes people reevaluate what the really important things in life really are. And the most important thing to me right now is making things "right" with my God and my Eternal companion. Darls I know that the Lord loves us both and he *knows of the good that the both of us can do in the world by our example to others. I honestly believe that this is the trial that will bolster our testimony and our faith to the extent that the blessings that have been pronounced upon us will come to pass in our lives. Darla I love you dearly, you are the one I'll spend forever with. Oh how lucky I am!!* ☺

Loving You for all Eternity,

Joe

I tried to remember if I'd ever heard Joe cuss. *No, I never did.* It amazed me that he didn't even slip when surrounded by those who didn't even try to hold back. I felt bad that I'd let one out when Jasmine got paint on J.R.'s furniture. I smiled as I recalled Jasmines random question at the dinner table about a month later, "Mommy, can I say d___?

After I responded with "No, I'd rather you not," she shot back with, "Well, you said it, Mommy!"

After Joe died, one of the soldiers in his company told me that Captain Reed was trying to help him clean up his language. I asked him if he was successful and the soldier laughed and said, "No, but he sure tried."

I'm truly the lucky one, Joe.

First grade was hard for J.R. It seemed he was figuring out that other kids had a dad and he didn't. I think he was also understanding a little more about what death meant. He wasn't interested in doing his work, learning how to read, or listening to the teacher. He often came home with notes from the teacher: "J.R. did not finish his work," "J.R. is daydreaming," "J.R. had trouble listening today." I explained to her what had happened, but she didn't seem to have any sympathy for him. Maybe she just didn't know what to do with him, so she continued to inform me on what J.R. wasn't doing. The school counselor suggested we get him tested for Attention Deficiency Disorder (ADD). I told her I was pretty sure he was grieving. She shook her head and continued to discuss the symptoms of ADD. It seemed she really wanted my son to have this condition.

We made an appointment with a psychologist. He called both of us in together and began asking me about my life and about J.R.'s dad. As I explained my husband's death, in detail because he asked specific questions, J.R. got antsy. This so-called expert then proceeded to tell me that my son obviously had ADD because he couldn't sit still while we were talking. We were talking about his father's death for crying out loud! I had J.R. go sit in the waiting room while I let this doctor know what I thought of his ridiculous diagnosis. What six year old would sit still during such a difficult discussion? How dare he put my son through that!

After this situation, I decided I would not go to anymore "experts." J.R. had shared with me what he was daydreaming about. It was always about his father and him going on different adventures. So we made a book with one of the stories, which was about him and his dad going to the moon and saving the world from a space monster. This made him really happy. I did "Hooked on Phonics" with him and got a tutor. Mamie was able to contact a classmate of Joe's, who was now an elementary school teacher. I wish Janae could have been his teacher at school as well as his tutor. She was so sweet with J.R., and he responded to someone who really cared.

I had to make a hard decision at the end of the school year. Should I hold him back or not? The principal suggested a special class for him. The class was for advanced kindergarten and first grade students, and the teacher adapted the curriculum to the level of the student's ability. As I visited the class and observed the teacher, I knew she was just who J.R. needed. She was kind and personable and addressed each child with interest. I will be forever grateful to Mrs. Moller. She was an angel and a perfect example of how teachers should be. J.R. got a new type of note sent home that next year: "You make me smile! You are super! You did great today!" He was proud of himself and wanted to do his work for her. (All teachers, please take note.)

The first time J.R. made a comment about his dad having died, Mrs. Moller consulted with me to know how I would want her to handle it. We set up a meeting with both of us and the school counselor. The teacher explained that every day, the students were supposed to write in their journals about different subjects. Instead of writing a whole page about how he got to school, J.R.wrote: "My dad did not drive me to school." J.R. also made comments about his father's death when the other students were sharing fun things about their lives. The school counselor thought J.R. had a writing disability and she went on to describe how people with this disability have to get someone to write for them. She also brought up A.D.D. again, and medication. I really wanted her to leave. I expressed my opinion that I thought this seven-year-old boy was trying to get out of writing and was playing the card he thought would work, but that I also wanted him to be able to write about his dad occasionally. The teacher and I came up with a plan: J.R. could write about his daddy one day per week, and he had to write a whole page just like all the other days. The counselor said something really stupid at one point. She asked if J.R. talked about his dad and his loss at home. I said that his little sister,

Jasmine expressed herself more about it than J.R. did. She then asked how old she was when her dad died. When I said sixteen months, she asked, "How can she be missing her daddy, she never even knew him?" Where did she get her degree? I wanted to know! She must not have had any experience with the death of a loved one. I really worried about how many kids were messed up because of this counselor! Later in the year she put J.R. in a group discussion with children who had experienced divorce! Despite the counselor, and with the help of Mrs. Moller, J.R. became a successful student that year.

Joe's family continued to provide so much love and support. They continued to help the children feel a connection with their father as they told them stories and told them how much they looked like their daddy. The kids loved Mamie's stories about her boy protecting his sisters on the bus, doing wheelies on his bike and going to dances dressed in his "Saturday Night Fever" suit. Pop would have us cracking up as he told the story of when Joe got into trouble all week long and then went to the neighbors (an older gentleman) to ask for advice on how to stop getting into so much trouble.

When the children were playing, we would also have discussions about their son's death, and how it has affected them. Pop shared how strange it is for him to have his son go somewhere he hasn't been.

Mamie felt like she should have been able to protect him or prevent what had happened. Sometimes, after talking to Mamie about her son, I would feel like we were grieving for two different people; her – for her little boy, and me – for my invincible super man. I would come back home so anxious to get the kids to bed and reacquaint myself with the confident, strong man I knew. I would drink up the letters from him, thirsty for any drop speaking straight to me now. He always delivered some morsel of precious reminder of who he was and still is and of his love and devotion for me.

My Dearestest Darla,   *27 Jan 91*

Today's Sunday, the Sabbath, however out in the field it feels just like any other work day! It is hard to believe that the rest of the church world wide are attending their meetings and resting from most of their labors. Today I'm going to take crackers and water and administer the sacrament to myself. Then I'll read some more scriptures for my talk and study a lesson out of the Priesthood manual.

Well I don't think I'm going to get to call you for awhile. We leave for combat early Tuesday morning. It sure was nice to talk to you the other day. It was a spur of the moment thing and I had to take advantage of it. Kevin did not get through to Kris, so he was bummin' hard! Although I do believe that he went to call her today! As far as the rest of my platoon is concerned, they are all taking things rather well despite the fact that they have not received any mail yet. Only a few of my soldiers have received anything with their name on it. Unfortunately the mail addressed to "Any Service member" takes priority over personal mail; which is ludicrous. We have plenty of this type of mail to go around, but very little personal stuff.

I have found that my platoon is poorly trained and not as disciplined as I would like. It is hard to make drastic changes now, so I've been letting a few things slide in order to maintain a relaxed atmosphere in the presence of an impending combat situation. All I can do now is pray and use the skills that I have at my disposal.

Hopefully by now you've heard the tape and read my last letter. I meant everything I said and wrote. You mean so very much to me and I realize how important you are in my life, as the days go by. I'm so proud of you and how well you are doing and taking all of this ordeal... You are definitely setting an example for a lot of other people.

Thanks for keeping in touch with my parents, and thank your parents for me as well; I definitely appreciate their concern for my parents, too! Please tell all that I love them and miss them and that I'm looking forward to seeing everyone soon.

But most importantly I'm looking forward to being with my beloved wife so that together we can raise up a righteous family to love and serve our Heavenly Father!

I Love you Sweetheart! Take care of yourself & our Home!

Loving you Eternally,

Joe

You did what was right even when it was hard. I need to train our "troops", to teach them discipline. It's okay to let some things slide huh, Joe? I hope you're still proud of me. Yes,

I'm keeping in touch with your parents. (Smile) Please be with me to raise up a righteous family, I need your help, Joe.

My journal:

Hi Babes,   *April 2000*

My mom is here for the week. We went to the beach and to Animal Kingdom with the kids. Tonight we watched "Run Away Bride." Cute movie. It made me want to fall in love. And when they were dancing I thought of how we used to dance together under the stars. You knew I loved that. You come into the picture every time I day dream about someone caring for me, someone rescuing me from having to take care of everything, my security, my knight in shining armor. When I really long for companionship, you are the only one I can ever imagine being there. After four years of no contact I am still madly in love with you and all I can do is hold onto the memories and be prepared for the day when we are reunited. I miss you tonight. But when I went in to check on the children, there was your pouty mouth when you slept, and your long dark eye lashes, and your beautiful brown skin, your chin, and your jaw line. You are all over our children. My love grows for you as it grows for your beautiful children.

When Jessica was four, she went to Little Fishes Preschool three times a week, from 9:00 to noon. Between picking her up and when my elementary school kids arrived home, I was anxious to get certain things done. I had a list of things to do and I expected her to cooperate with me as I rushed her to the car. Most days, she had her own agenda. One day she ran out to a small open grassy area and squatted down to inspect the ground. I could barely see a hint of color among the grass and weeds. She stood and squatted many times as I pled for her to come. She finally ran over to me and presented me with a miniscule bouquet of flowers, "Flowers for you, Mommy!"

"Thank you Jessi. They are so beautiful!"

This became her routine when I picked her up. The first few times I waited very impatiently. While I watched her I would be thinking of all the errands I needed to run before her brother and sister got home. I didn't want to run them with three kids in tow. I would usually cut the flower collecting short by calling to her, "Okay, that's enough, let's go. We have so much to do!"

One day I watched her with different eyes. I had gone to the temple that morning. Going to the temple always made me slow down and remember what was most important in life. I watched her little hands very carefully plucking up the strands of green. I saw her inspect each flower, sometimes throwing one down. I saw her very carefully push the one stem into her other hand with the bouquet she had started. This seemed to be difficult for her little hands to accomplish. I watched her little body in a squatting position, her curls blowing in the wind, not worrying about time. Her only goal was to make her mommy happy with flowers. Her little legs stood and squatted many times before she came running and smiling, "Mommy, Mommy, I got flowers for you!"

She presented them like it was the first time she had ever done it and I squatted down to be eye to eye with my precious Jessica. I was more sincere this time as I thanked her for the flowers, and I looked at them, but not as weeds this time. I inspected these miniature flowers in my hand. They were not weeds at all, but were beautiful flowers. I was surprised with their beauty. How could something so small have such detail? I hugged my sweet little girl, realizing moments like this won't last forever and I must cherish them.

I like to make analogies. Some nights after

getting the children to bed I'd sit in my "formal" front room. I had a second-hand couch on one wall and a shelf with toys in baskets on the other. The rest of the space was used for indoor baseball, racing, dancing, setting up a tent...etc. I liked to sit on the couch and stare into space, as I was frequently overwhelmed by my reality. My formal dining room had a vaulted ceiling, it was beautiful and I was amazed with it. The house seemed bigger from that couch. That night as I sat there, replaying the day in my head, I saw my little Jessica picking flowers for me. I was in such a hurry all the time, I fought my fowl mood, and I wanted things to go smoothly. I had an agenda. I often thought of how hard my life was. I saw a field of weeds and Jessica saw flowers. I thought of how my challenges seem like an endless field of weeds, and I am often overwhelmed by the work involved with clearing them. But if I follow Jessica's example, I can look closer and see the flowers: my three beautiful children, the support and love from friends and family, the strength that I've gained, the closer I've become to God, and the insight He has given me. I resolved again to slow down and look for the flowers.

My Wonderful Wife,   *30 Jan. '91*

Well today we went to do a rehearsal of our mission. I cannot believe how much teamwork and coordination it takes to pull off major operations like this, it is incredible.

The weather here has gotten better, though it is close to freezing in the early mornings. Usually the sun warms things up between 0900-1000. Nevertheless everyone is walking around here with colds and runny noses. The Egyptians and Syrians have set a whole lot of ammunition and other equipment in front of our positions. It is obvious that in their cultures they are not used to having thieves around because they leave all of their stuff unguarded. They come by every now and then when they are left without food or water. It appears as though they plan on being here for a very long time from the way they have things set up.

We are told that after we've kicked Saddam out of Kuwait and destroyed a major part of his Army we'll be sent home and the Arab nations will be the peace keeping force! Have I told you this already? Any ways from the way things look and from what we are told that is the plan.

Oh by the way I managed to really screw up today by leaving my Kevlar Helmet at the rehearsal site this morning. When I went back to look for it sometime later it was gone. I'm hoping that someone picked it up or else I'm up the creek. Hopefully if it doesn't turn up I can get another one.

No, I haven't received any mail yet!! The mail system is really screwed up here for 1st Inf. Div. Although I do not understand why you have not received mail! Most of my men have not received mail either except for a few isolated cases where the soldiers have wives or relatives over here too. I'm not as concerned now because I have a lot on my mind, but there are those lonely evenings when all I can think of is being with you! Sometimes I can almost visualize what it will be like to have our first child. Most of the time I think of playing with him or her when I get home from work just before we sit down to eat dinner. That is one of my dreams!! And I hope and pray that that day will come soon!

Have I told you how far along I am

in the Book of Mormon? Just this morning I finished Alma's sermon to the Zoramites about "Faith" and comparing it to a seed! Tonight I'm going to get through Alma 40. What I want to do is finish the B of M and then go straight into the New Testament and do some comparisons especially with the four Gospels. After that I'm going to get a better grasp on the D & C and P of GP. If I'm not home by then, then I'll tackle the Old Testament. My goal is to get through all of the Standard Works this year so that I can have a better knowledge of the big picture. Then I'd like to <u>study</u> things in parts to get a better feel of how the Gospel reinforces itself over & over through the different Prophets. I think that this approach will help me to be more adept with the scriptures, especially the Bible.

Darls, I love you dearly and I sincerely hope that you are doing well. Take Care Babes!

Yours For All Eternity,

Joe

As I read this letter I could imagine Joe telling me to chill out and appreciate being able to play with our children. I imagined him being frustrated when watching me lose my temper with them and pass up fleeting moments as I rushed around. I promised him that I would hold our babies tight enough for the both of us.

Jasmine got an easel for her birthday. I put it on the porch and put her little apron on her. She was so excited to paint. She was jumping up and down and giggling as I took the lid off each bottle: red, yellow, blue, and green.

"Wait!" I stopped her before she dunked the paint brush in the first bottle, "I want you to paint a pretty picture on the big piece of paper. Do not paint the easel. Do not paint yourself. Do not paint the walls of our house. If you do, you will not get to paint again for a very, very long time."

Her chin was tilted down and her eyes were up at me as she said, "Okay Mommy."

"Do you understand the consequence?" I asked.

"No painting for a very, very long time." She stared and then asked, "How long Mommy?"

I randomly selected a time, "A month….that is

30 days…can you count to 30?"

"Yes Mommy, it's a lot of days!"

"Okay Jasmine, you have fun and I'll be back to check on you." I went off to do dishes and what not, and then came back on the porch to check on her. I gasped! Jasmine's face, legs, and arms were covered with paint. She had used all the colors but not one speck of paint was on the apron and only one line of red paint was on the paper in front of her.

She turned and immediately and calmly stated, with paint brush in hand, "I'll take the consequence."

The greeting on Joe's letter alone was enough to make up for the craziness of the day.

My Dearest Princess,   *04 Feb. '91*

I must be crazy writing you when I know that these letters are not getting to you. However I feel better when I've at least tried to talk to you. I think I'm going to try to call you tomorrow. Obviously I've not left from the last place I told you about. Right now I'm listening to Luther Vandross In Concert and watching my platoon engage in a friendly game of touch football. Lately we've had some problems with discipline in the platoon. These guys have never had someone demand the respect and discipline that a soldier ought to display. They are learning quickly that I don't play those games. (Homey don't play dhat!) There has been nothing too serious yet, and I'm hoping that there won't be. I'd hate to have to exercise my authority over them in an environment that is already uncomfortable.

Oh guess what? One of the other platoon leaders, Rob Mitchell, received the sound track the "Little Mermaid" from his girlfriend. This morning he loaned it to me, so I've been sitting here listening to Sebastian the crab sing, "Kiss the Girl"! Do you know that at night I lay in my sleeping bag and dream about kissing you? Yep I sure do! They are the same dreams I had while you were away on your mission. I really used to be hurting then; because that was all we could do! You remember the old rule book don't you? I sure am glad that that is behind us now because . . . it would not be as much fun with rules!!

So how are you doing at work? Have

you tried to certify as an aerobic instructor yet? I sure hope you do those types of things so that can be on your resume in the future. I also hope that school is going well too! You said you were taking biology, so that ought to be interesting.

I wish this mail situation would get better because I feel as though I'm writing you and telling you the same things over and over again. Everyone else is sucking it down pretty bad as well. I'd give almost anything to get even a post card from someone I knew. The news situation is somewhat better though. At least we hear some of what is going on in the war and at home. The only news I really want to know is that my dear sweet wife is doing well and that her immediate needs are being met. I pray that things are going well at home and that Heavenly Father is sending his Spirit to help you during these days while we are apart. I Love you sweetheart and I can't wait to come home and be with you forever! Take good care and tell all I said "Hello"!

> Loving You For All Eternity,
> Joe

Do angels' prayers get priority? I wonder.

I took the girls to the grocery store with me. Jessica wanted to ride, Jasmine wanted to push, and as usual, I was in a hurry. I decided I could leave them with the cart at the end of each aisle while I ran to snatch the product I needed from the middle of the aisle. I noticed Jessica calling Jasmine, "Mommy."

"How cute," I thought as I rushed through the store, periodically leaving them for a moment to run after an item.

When we were approaching the check-out, Jasmine told Jessica, "It's okay, you can stop calling me Mommy now."

I gave Jasmine an inquisitive look so she happily explained, "I was having Jessica call me Mommy so people would think I was a midget and they wouldn't take us."

My mom and I talked on the phone quite often. We liked to compare amazing manly-type jobs we had done. I thought I had her beat when I fixed the dryer all by myself! The only help I had was a phone-a-repairman service. The guy laughed when he heard the sound my dryer was making! He talked me through taking the whole front section off, finding the problem and putting it back together. I was so proud and felt like I could do anything! But Mom seemed to outdo me most of the time. When I called to brag about my dryer, she was laying her own flagstone in the back yard, for crying out loud!

I painted furniture, painted all the walls in the house, and refinished our kitchen table. I always listened to a tape while I did my projects. I would either listen to Joe or inspirational messages or books on tape. It was good therapy for me.

I was very proud of my 6.5 horse power mower. It used to take me an hour to mow that Florida St. Augustine grass but with my new power machine I brought it down to twenty minutes! All the neighborhood men were envious of my mower. My favorite phrase was something I learned on my mission from a cute little Argentinean woman (the same one who furnished daily patisseries). When we visited her, she would play show-and-tell with all the things she had made or decorated. She would smile and say "tout ca, c'est moi qui la fait!" It means, "All of this, it's me who did it!" My mother learned the phrase too. I would stand and admire my work and say the phrase out loud and I would smile and feel empowered.

I was also ready to fight verbally with anyone who would challenge me! This actually started way back in the anger stage. The month my father died I forgot to pay my car payment. I didn't catch it until April when I realized I was being charged for every day I was late and they were counting every payment to be thirty days late. The first guy I talked to pompously responded with, "I paid all my bills when my father died!" What a schmuck! I went above his head and didn't get much further. I ended up making my way up to the president of the bank and when he stated that this was the bank's policy, I asked him if he could sleep at night taking money from a fatherless widow! This was after reviewing my amazing payment record previous to this incident. He was silent for a while and then asked me if I thought it would be fair if I was charged for the first month I was late, and I said, "Yes." After I hung up I clenched my fists and proclaimed, "Don't mess with Widow Reed!" And I've continued with this attitude!

As I was being forced to learn how to take care of everything, I became more and more impatient with women who had their husbands do everything for them. One time I asked a woman to take a picture of me and the kids when we were out and about. She said "Oh no, I can't take pictures. My husband always does that."

I contained my fury and nicely but firmly said, "You can do this. Take the camera and look through it and push this button!" She followed directions well and I have that picture today to prove how capable she was, thank you very much! No woman was going to be so pathetically dependent on her husband while I was around.

My Beautiful Bride,   *10 Feb 1991*

It seems as though lately all I can think of is you, especially since I've received the photos you sent me. I am so glad that we are receiving mail now that I anxiously await the mail runners to return each night with it. Also each night I go to sleep with you on my mind and in my dreams. Just like in Ranger School I've planned out all the things we are going to do and get when I return. Although I know we can't buy and do it all, it's sure nice dreaming about it.

Ya know yesterday I read through all of third Nephi, and I cried through the whole thing. It is such a great feeling when the Spirit touches your heart and enlightens your mind as you read the scriptures. I haven't felt that way since I left West Point while reading the scriptures. Then again I haven't devoted as much effort in scripture study as then either. I can see why it is important to get in the habit of scripture study at an appointed time of day, while you're young. Because as you grow older and are faced with more responsibilities and distractions you can definitely lose sight of the importance of regular scripture study. That is what happened to me last year. I got so caught up in work being married and other things (t.v.) that I kind of blew the scrips off.

In a way the time I have now to read ponder and pray is a blessing. I always felt a little cheated because I couldn't serve a mission and have that time to seriously study and apply the scriptures in everything I did! But now I'm going to take the time to read *only* scriptures. I'm making a conscious effort not to even read Tom Clancy or other books except military manuals. I'm sure however that I may read something else once the war is over.

Oh, before I forget, stick these extra pages of notes I took a long time ago in a safe place. I don't want to lose these by accident or get them mutilated. They are memoirs of some of my past thoughts.

Darls can I tell you that I think you're great!! I know I must tell you this every letter, but it's all true. Yesterday as I read in 3 Nephi where Jesus cries as he blesses the Nephite children I too cried. I thought of how close a new born baby is to the Savior as he is brought into mortality from our Heavenly home. All I could think of is seeing our own new born child right after he enters the world, and saying to myself, " I will do and teach you everything in my power to get you back to your Heavenly home."

I have so many thoughts like this that I wish I could share with you in person, but I guess this is how it must be for now.

So Tim has a new job huh! That is great for he and Danette. With Dale getting off his mission in 10 days, I'm sure your folks will feel the ease of not having another financial burden on their hands. Also with Dale home it will give your family something to rally behind as he gets his life put back together. It should be fun watching him catch up on music, current events, and of course, the female dilemma!! Tell him I said, "Good luck"!

Please let me know how the income tax return situation goes. I'm sure things will be different now that we are married. The government will probably want more money from us. Speaking of money call my Dad and ask him to find out if the interest rate on our credit cards goes down because of my deployment in a war. He should be able to get some good info on the subject.

Well Sweetheart it is about time for me to mail this letter, so I need to close it off. I just found out some discouraging news yesterday that I know you will not like. Starting tomorrow @ noon the telephones will be off limits due to the nearness of the ground forces engaging in the war. I think the higher echelon leaders are trying to limit the possibility of valuable information getting into the wrong hands via the telephones. Please inform my parents that I am sorry that I did not get a chance to call before this happened, but tell them I love them and I think about *them daily. There are also letters coming to them as well.*

Be good Babes, and Take care of yourself and our <u>home</u>!

Loving You Eternally,

Joe

A few times Joe asked me to take care of our home as well as myself as he closed his letters. When he was writing me, I was in an apartment we would never live in together and we didn't have any children. Was he talking about our finances and our car? I wondered if he was inspired to give me a message that would be significant to me much later when I would be responsible for our children, our family—our home. I took his request very seriously.

The notes he wanted me to put in a safe place proved to contain some of the most precious words from my husband. Many women in the church are privileged to have their husband or father give them a blessing in times when they are struggling physically, mentally or spiritually. Because he jotted down his thoughts, I can now be reminded of blessings past and be strengthened. It is also a reminder of what his goals were as I try to "take care of our home."

Establishing the Home

-Immediately give Darla a blessing

-Dedicate our house to be a family Temple (our own kingdom) a place of order & organization; that the spirit will abide there constantly, because it will be centered in Christ and glow with the Gospel principles; that it will be an oasis wherewith our family can feel safe and unafraid because of the peacefulness it will emanate.

Darla's Blessing

-Give blessing to establish this new (kingdom) family that through its faithfulness that the Lord will be well pleased.

-Bless Darla and set her apart to be the counselor and conductor of the affairs of this family.

-As a wife to be able to discern the needs of her husband because they are many. To administer to him with love and faithfulness in his trials, to never doubt

him. Bless her with patience that she may be able to endure the many trials that await her as a wife and mother. And that she may endure the comments and situations she will be placed in by others.

-Bless her to use her knowledge of the Gospel along with its principles and precepts to help keep the family in line with the Lord's program.

-Bless her with strength and courage to take hold of the responsibilities left vacant at times while her husband is away.

He had no idea what was coming and how precious these thoughts would be. They continue to give me strength every time I read them.

I know Joe is our guardian angel, or as we call it in the Church—our administering angel. If he was busy I was sure that he would send other family members. Maybe my dad filled in for him or great grandparents or other family members who had passed on.

When Jessica was about eighteen months old I put her in her crib for the night. Not much time had passed when I heard a crashing noise. I came rushing in to find Jessica under the dresser that had fallen forward. The little rascal had managed to climb out of her crib and then she had attempted to climb the dresser!

I quickly lifted it up and looked for injuries as I asked, "Where's the owie, Jessi?" I just knew I would be rushing her to the emergency room with broken bones.

She pushed my arms away and said "No owie!" I continued to investigate but found nothing wrong with her. The doctor examined her the next day. Not even a bruise was found. I looked to the heavens and whispered, "Thanks Babe."

Around that same time, the kids were all playing outside and J.R. got the brilliant idea to open the garage and ride it up. When it got to his waist he grabbed onto the bottom and when it stopped at the top he jumped down. What fun! Jessica decided it was her turn! She rode all the way up and then Jasmine decided to help her down by holding her feet, so now instead of falling to her feet, she fell face first with her feet in Jasmine's hands. I came out to find Jessica crying and her lip bleeding just a bit. Once I heard what had happened, I was sure there was at least one angel keeping her from having her teeth all knocked out!

Years later, I was putting my mascara on while driving to church. Yes, I know I can be quite stupid. Barricades were lining the street where construction was taking place, and Jasmine was in the front seat with the window down. A sudden loud pop almost made my heart stop. I pulled over immediately to find out what had happened. The side mirror on the passenger's side was hanging down with the mirror missing. The glass from the mirror was all on the floor of the van and on the dash board in front of my daughter. As I examined Jasmine, the only glass I found on her was a small speck in her eyelash. The more I thought about what happened as my side mirror hit the barricade, I couldn't figure out how the glass did not end up all over my daughter. Maybe some physics expert will explain how it could happen, but I chalk it up as an amazing miracle that my husband had something to do with. If Joe had sent someone else to protect us that day, I imagined them saying, "I quit! Your wife is crazy! It's too much work to keep your family safe!" I thanked the heavens for this blessing and vowed to be a safer driver.

Jessica ended up in my bed quite often. One morning, when she was around two, I was reading and she was sound asleep by my side. She suddenly sat up and yelled, "Daddy!" She then ran around to my side of the bed to the picture I kept there and said, "Daddy, that's my daddy, he talk to me!"

"What did he say, Sweetie?"

"He say I wove you and I be wight back!"

"What else did he say?"

"That's all!" She then took off racing around the house and I couldn't get her to elaborate or talk about it again.

My Dear Sweet Wife,   15 *Feb* 1991

The past few days have been extremely hectic. We have moved closer and closer to the Kuwaiti Border each day. Tomorrow we move to our position just short of the border. There have been many reports of defectors surrendering to the Allied Forces all along the border. Many of them have been in our sector.

Today we heard over the radio that Saddam was willing to pull out of Kuwait given certain conditions. It's too bad that we demand an unconditional surrender and withdrawal from Kuwait. From where we are, at night we can see and hear the bombs hitting targets along the border. These people are in a seriously hurting situation.

Their sewage structure in Baghdad has been ruptured, they have no electricity, and food is scarce. Saddam is definitely insane.

Well I hope that all is well with you and the home front. I haven't received any mail since last week when I got the care packages. Hopefully you are receiving my mail. I'd feel much better knowing that you are at least hearing from me. I especially hope that you received your Valentines card. Last year was my first year receiving a Valentines card from someone I really was in love with. Yep, it was pretty darn special. What I wouldn't give to be sharing Valentine's Day with you . . .Anyways tomorrow is Saturday and we are supposed to get mail. I sure could use some mail from my #1 girl.

I finally finished the B of M today. Ya know I don't think I've ever read the Book of Ether in it's entirety before. It covers such a large span of time that it is hard to follow who begat who and who reigned after who. Nevertheless I got a lot out of it and I plan to go back and study that particular book in the B of M before I dive into the N.T. I am in the process of rereading Jacob 5 to put the Lord's plan of preserving his people into clearer focus. I think it will help me to understand more about the New Testament.

Probably the two biggest principles that I gained a better understanding of are the principle of "repentance", and then how repentance extends the law of mercy over the laws of justice. Being humbled as I am now in this situation and these living conditions, I have found it easier to repent of things past and present. I suppose when the possibility of leaving this life is much greater, a person strives to become as clean as possible.

Hey, do you know what? I love you so much that I could just bust open with joy. Every night I lay awake for awhile just thinking of what it feels like to hold you close in the early morning hours. I miss that feeling so much that often I reach my arm out to pull you close, but there's no Darla. ☹ Like right now, I'm listening to Luther sing our Wedding Song, just dreaming of being with you. I *have to pull out the pictures of us everyday to give myself a recharge and assurance that you are really mine and that everything will be fine. I know I write this every letter, but I can't wait to come home, start a family and enjoy...you!!! I love you Sweetheart! Take care!*

Yours For All Eternity,

Joe

I know about hectic days! Okay, they're nothing in comparison to war, I can't relate. I can relate with missing you holding me though, I ache for that feeling. Maybe I can will myself to dream about you. Good night, Babes. I love you too.

I've been asked by other single mothers who are widowed or divorced, "When were you able to feel happy?" That's a hard one to answer. I think that as time passed, I was able to have more happy moments and less sad moments. It was a process, not like I can say, "Yes, exactly three years after he died, I was able to be happy again." I cried a little less and laughing came a little easier as the days rolled into years.

As quite a few years have passed I've noticed my

ability to feel extreme joy over very simple things. I think that the happiness I can feel now is more profound because I have felt such a profound sorrow. I first thought of this when driving a convertible. The weather was perfect and the scenery was beautiful and I had, "To Where You Are," by Josh Groban cranked up so high as to drown out my bad singing. Such a simple thing, but I was feeling pure joy and pure gratitude for every aspect of that moment.

I've also realized what it means to have faith in Christ and what He meant when He said, "Come unto me...and ye shall find rest to your souls." I did have some moments while praying when I felt my sadness and anger taken away and a peace fill my heart. I had a hope that I didn't always see in everyone else in my situation. With time I was able to see that the Lord had lightened my burden even though He didn't take it all away. I could see that His influence in my life helped me not to worry and to feel safe, something I took for granted until hearing others express their worries. I now know with all my heart, that my faith in the Lord and my understanding of His gospel does a whole lot more for me than to just help me look forward to my death more than others. It helps me to feel pure happiness.

CHAPTER 14

Carrying On

I lived in Florida by Mamie and Pop for almost six years. They supplied a lot of fun moments for the children at a crucial time in their lives. I used to get overwhelmed with the task of thinking of a fun activity for them. Mamie had the best Easter egg hunts in their back yard with our neighborhood friends. The kids would find more than eggs hidden in her trees; she loved to hide gifts as well. It used to amaze me the way a simple game of memory would feel like the Olympics with the energy they would put into it. They had regular dinner parties in their home and the children would be the host and hostess', greeting the guests, taking their coats and leading them to the back porch. Then they would become the entertainment for the crowd. Jessica would sing, Jasmine would do ballet or tell a story and J.R. would do a Tae Kwon Do routine. Their confidence level would soar as the whole party would erupt in applause and praise.

They had a great group of friends who made us feel welcomed and loved. I will forever be grateful for them as well as for Vonda and Daria, who joined in on adding a lot of love and happy moments to our lives.

I attended many formal events and parties with them. We went on trips to South Carolina and Jersey to see family. I love Joe's whole family. My grandparents died when I was young, so I was grateful to have Big Mama and Granddaddy, and Nanny and Pop Pop, for the kids as well as myself. I know it added to the kids' feeling of security and belonging, as they could feel the love everyone has had for them.

In June of 2002 I moved us to Arizona to be close to my family. It was a prayerful decision. I felt the need of having the religious support my family could give me.

It was so hard to leave my in-laws and all the hands-on support they gave me. It was hard to leave my good friends and neighbors, Kim and Bob. We were constantly in each other's pantries and had kids running back and forth between our homes. Kim was better than a GPS. I called her regularly when I was lost. It was also hard to leave my dear friend, Agnes. I'm glad we still get together whenever we can and we check on each other on a weekly basis. I felt sad about leaving the cemetery where Joe's grave site is. I miss going and talking to him there. There were so many other people and things I miss about Florida, but as hard as it was to leave, I knew it was what was best for us at that time.

The summer before we moved, I took the kids to DC to attend a TAPS seminar together. This was the seminar after 9-11. I will always remember an exchange I had with another woman in the hotel elevator. This scenario was a great example of what goes on at the seminars. Just the two of us were in the elevator:

"Are you here for the TAPS seminar?" I asked.

"Yes, my husband was in the Pentagon on 9-11"

"I'm so sorry for your loss." I replied.

"Are you a widow also?"

"Yes, my husband was killed in a training accident. It's been six years."

"Wow, that much time, I can't imagine." She paused and then quietly asked "Does it get any easier?"

I thought for a moment because of everything I

had been through during those six years. She had so much to deal with and so much to feel. But yes, I could honestly say, yes, it does get easier; easier to smile and to laugh and easier to remember without crying and easier to do day to day things without thinking about your loss. We both gained something in that small interaction in the elevator. She was given hope for a brighter day and I was reminded of how far I've come.

After the seminar we flew up to New York. I felt a rush of joy as I drove the rented car on the Hutch (the Hutchinson River Parkway) on my way to visit the Coopers. I love New York. Terry and Doug were the same. Josh and Abby weren't! They were now young adults. At one point Joshua was playing catch with J.R., and Abby was making cookies with the girls in the kitchen, the same activities I had done with them so many years ago. I still felt at home in their presence.

We drove up to West Point the next day. So many memories of this drive filled my mind: my first accident in the round-about, Joe in his uniform, parades and dances, Bear Mountain, where Joe proposed. Now we were going up to take part in the annual presentation of the Kurkowski-Reed Excellence in Engineering psychology award. Joe and the other cadet named, who also passed away, graduated with this major. This award is given out in their memory and they are always appreciative when family can participate and personalize the ceremony. We were treated as honored guests from the moment we entered the gate. Two cadets took us on a tour of West Point. Our tour guides were really sweet with the children as they showed them where their dad lived, ate, and studied. During the award ceremony, before I handed the award to the top engineer student, I was given the opportunity to say a few words about my husband.

Here's what I shared:

> On Joe's last evaluation report it says: "Willing to stand up for what is right." Joe Reed stood up for what was right whether anyone was watching or not. I've never met anyone with more integrity than Joe. A good example is when he decided to get certified as a jump master. Every night he practiced as he prepared for this test, physically going through all the checks he would do on a jumper and his parachute before he exited the plane. And then, holding onto the doorway of our bedroom, he would look out as if he were poking his head out of the doorway of the plane, making the noise of the wind as he checked the sides and the ground below.

He was confident and anxious to get that patch put on his uniform. I was very surprised when he came through the door that night with disappointment written all over his face. I was even more surprised and confused when he announced that he had passed the test. He explained that a man who was testing him, pointed at one of the spots he was supposed to check. Even though Joe knew the routine, he felt like it would be wrong to accept the patch because this man had "helped" him. He also knew that if he turned this man in, he could ruin his career. He stewed over this for days. He lost sleep over it, and he prayed about it. He phoned his friends whom he respected, for their advice. So many people would not have worried about it. His friends advised him to let it go because he knew the material and had not cheated. After a few days of contemplation, Joe chose not to wear the patch. He said he could not wear it with a clear conscience. This still amazes me. He was all about the values that are stressed at West Point: "Duty, Honor, Country" and "I will not lie, cheat, or steal, or tolerate those who do."

It felt good to be able to share that story with

those who truly understood the values taught at the academy. After the ceremony, we went to watch the cadets in the parade field. I sobbed silently as I sat behind my children in the bleachers. This was way too much for my heart to take as I had so many memories of watching Joe stand tall and proud in his uniform as he marched on this very field. He was so much a part of this place. He had embraced the traditions of strength, integrity, character and courage. Though it broke my heart to be there without Joe, I didn't want to leave. We wandered around the academy for a few hours more until I had worn us all out.

From West Point we went on to visit family in Jersey; Nanny, Aunt Anna Mae, Uncle Harold, Auntie Lillian, Uncle Danny, cousins David, Darrell and Donna, great aunts and uncles. Joe has a lot of family on the Jersey Shore.

I really enjoyed my visit with Nanny though she was very sad that I was moving to Arizona. She had planned to move to Florida since her health was getting worse and Pop Pop had died the year before. It broke my heart to disappoint her. Late that night we discussed my religion and what we did in the temple and why Joe sacrificed so much to be married there. As we discussed her and Pop Pop's relationship and how she would want to be with him again, she said she would be grateful for me to have her and

Pop Pop sealed after she passed on. It was a sweet moment with her that I will cherish. I have found great joy in showing my love for his family by doing this work for them in the temple.

When we were saying goodbye the next morning I felt very emotional and had a strange feeling that it would be the last time I would see her. But I still had hopes of spending more time with her when we returned to Florida for Christmas. The first feeling I had proved to be right, Nanny passed away the following November.

The organization called TAPS has played a huge role in our lives. A couple years after I attended my first TAPS seminar I started taking the kids so that they could benefit from them. They all had a turn to go with me by themselves, when they were around seven years old. They have a program called "The Good Grief Camp," which really helped the children to feel proud of their dad and what he did for our country. It was great for them to meet other kids their age who were dealing with the same type of loss and to have many people (counselors, volunteer Honor Guard, generals, celebrities and politicians) talk to them and thank them for their fathers' service.

Besides the emotional benefits of the seminars, TAPS gave us so many amazing opportunities. Really, it is Bonnie Carroll, the founder who I have to thank. Because of her, Jessica was privileged to present the TAPS wreath at the Tomb of the Unknown Soldier when she first went to the Memorial Day Seminar in 2003. Jasmine was able to participate in President Bush's Inauguration at the military gala when she was ten (Jan. 2004). She stood before 15,000 people, including the president of the United States, and said her dad's name and the date of his death. While waiting for her turn on stage she invited Gloria Estefan to join her at the next TAPS seminar since Gloria's dad's death was related to military service. She presented TAPS coins to Kelsey Grammer and BeBe Winans and others. As she handed the TAPS coin to former President George H. W. Bush, he said he wished he had something to give her. She responded with, "A hug will do." So she got a hug from him, as well as Barbara and Laura Bush. I was so impressed with my daughter. I probably would've giggled nervously and said something stupid, but Jaz had just the right thing to say. Jasmine also had a little TAPS doll named after her that same year. In 2005, Bonnie had Jessica sing The "Star Spangled Banner" and "God Bless America" at the Memorial Day seminar, while pictures of her daddy flashed on a screen beside her. That same year Jasmine wrote a poem that Bonnie put in the TAPS magazine and she was able to read it during the formal banquet at the seminar. A few years later, Jessica and I were both flown to DC for her to sing the "National Anthem" at a TAPS gala. Because of my association with TAPS, I was able to help change the educational benefits for military widows in December of 2005. The time to utilize funds for a four-year degree used to be ten years. Now, with the change, widows have twenty years. I wrote a letter describing why a widow would need more time and Eddie Smith, who Bonnie introduced me to, helped get the letter to the right senators. Eddie called me when it passed and said that I must have someone from up above looking out for me because these things don't usually go through so quickly. Yes, I could think of a couple angels who had my back.

Recently the girls and I received the royal treatment as we were flown up to Las Vegas to attend the Miss America Pageant, thanks to our relationship with TAPS. This special weekend was compliments of some very giving, kind-hearted women, Darci Hansen and former Miss America, Sharlene Wells Hawkes.

Along with trials come the blessings. I'm so grateful for all of these amazing experiences for my children which have replaced sadness with patriotism and pride in the legacy their father left behind. This last experience was very humbling for me as we were showered with gifts and services from so many people. I can't thank Bonnie enough for the amazing experiences she has provided for my family.

Through the TAPS program, I had learned that

children can go through the stages of grieving over and over again at different times in their lives. Even though I had learned this, I was still caught off guard when Jasmine started struggling with her dad's death during her fifth grade year. She wanted to listen to her daddy's tapes and she cried a lot. She would run out of class either to cry or because she had a headache. This happened almost every other day for a month or so. She went to Mrs. Birt, the school counselor, quite often. I appreciated her having someone else to talk to, who I knew I could trust. I had her go to a grieving camp in Prescott that spring and we went to TAPS that year—the year she was able to read her poem. She had written this poem the summer before she went through this difficult time. It was interesting that she now needed her own advice:

Carry It On
By Jasmine Reed

When someone leaves you that you love carry on their legacy carry it on.

Don't be so sad and give up, always remember to carry it on.

Treasure what they left behind then carry it on, carry it on.

I know it's hard without them,

But I know you can find the strength within to carry on carry on.

That loved one still is in you.

I see it every day as I watch you carry on, carry on.

They don't want to see you sad,

They want to see you happy while you carry on-

On what they have started.

So, have fun as you carry it on, carry it on.

Carry on the love and the joy as they peacefully rest

Carry it on, carry it on.

Cause when you carry it on

It makes the world a better place.

So carry it on, carry it on

Always remember to carry it on.

Jessica seemed to have similar feelings her sixth grade year. She needed to grieve for her loss and I tried to be there to hold her and listen. I dreaded the yearly father-daughter dance the elementary school would have. On the night of the dance we would either go out to dinner or they would go along with a friend and her father. Her sixth grade year, Pop was on a business trip in California and drove five hours to be able to accompany Jessica to the dance. Jasmine and I were out of town at a volleyball tournament so my mother was there with Jessica and J.R. for the weekend. Mom said Jessica didn't feel well and was worried she wouldn't be able to go, but when Pop came in the house, Jessica's face lit up and she ran and jumped into his arms. Pop said he was so tired and the thought of driving back the next morning was not something he was looking forward to, but seeing Jessica's reaction made it all worth it. They had a great time. *Thanks Pop.* I am grateful to share that both girls got past their stage of sadness and returned to their extremely cheerful selves.

As time passed, I referred to Joe's letters less frequently. I was going to school and trying to keep up with the kids' ever increasingly complicated schedules. It was on special dates, or moments when I was feeling overwhelmed, that I would pull the notebook out. I organized his letters from the war in order and placed them in paper protectors. Sometimes I would flip the pages just to look at the way he greeted me, and that alone would give me comfort and strength. After all these years, as infrequently as I've read them, I still find a bit of reassurance, comfort and advice from Joe and I am still amazed with the messages he has left for me and his posterity.

Sweetheart,   21 Feb 1991

Well 4 years ago today was a very special day in history. One of America's finest met Heaven's most gorgeous; thus the most powerful partnership in the universe was begun.

How's that for a storybook intro? Well it is true! However the partnership was not sealed in it's power until Jan 2 1990. Today must be a big day for all back in Arizona with Dale coming off his mission. Today I was supposed to take my platoon on a security mission across the border into Iraq, but the mission was just cancelled.

Hey I just got the best birthday present I could receive way out here, 2 letters from you! ☺ I also got a really great letter from J'Deene Parkhurst and a whole manila envelope full of cards and a computer banner from congregation at St. John's the Episcopal Church, which included letters from Mom & Daria.

I only wish that the letters were current so that I could know what you are up to now. The letters from you are dated 15 and 19 January and here it is 21 Feb. The mail system really sucks even if I am on the Front lines now. Any ways Babes, I really got a thrill out of seeing your lips on the back of the one letter. I want to kiss your lips so bad that I dream about it every night. It reminds me of how I dreamt about it and how it felt while you were on your mission. Continue to do it and also send some more of that soft musk. You have no idea of how much a morale booster that is for me. Smell effects while reading your letters and looking at your picture make me feel revitalized because I am that much closer to my eternal mate.

How are your parents? I'm going to try and get a letter off to them in a day or so. Tell your Dad that if he did send a knife, it will definitely come in handy. And send word to Adam White that I'm doing fine. [Adam was a boy in Willcox who Joe befriended.]

So how's Biology treating you? Hopefully you're excelling and setting the Natural Reed Standard of perfection. What about your institute class? ...I am amazed at how much faith some people have in the Lord. I am overwhelmed at how men and women of enormous stature and prestige can be so meek and lowly in heart. ...Every day I pray that I can lead these men RIGHTEOUSLY, which is hard to do when very few of them even believe in God, most of them use his Holy Name in vain like it was a by word like "it" . . .Faith out here is not a choice for it is all I really have!

Well now that my sermon has ended; how's work? Have you certified as an aerobics instructor yet? If you have not you'd better do it before I come home because when I get back in the states, BAM we are out of Tucson and Wham Bam you're pregnant!! ☺ So don't waste precious time putting anything off. Have you received a calling yet? Hopefully, like you said it will be a teaching calling, so you can study.

In this envelope, as you have seen, are "surrender leaflets" that we've been dropping on the Iraqis to get them to surrender peacefully before we bomb the you know what out of them. Because we are right up on the border they blow all over the place so I have picked them up every now & then. There are 3 different kinds 2 in color & 1 in black and white. Keep 1 of each kind for us and laminate them so we can preserve them as souvenirs. The rest give to the family as souvenirs of war.

Sweetheart I sure hope that you are getting my mail more often than I'm getting yours. It would be a great comfort to me knowing that at least you were hearing from me. I tell you that I love you all the time, but I know that is not enough. You need me to show you in actions and I want to do that so bad it hurts. But for now all I can do is tell you that I love you more & more every day. You're mine and you always will be no matter what. Take Good Care of yourself and our home.

Loving You Forever!

Your Eternal Companion,

Joe

CHAPTER 15

Always Near

Even though I haven't had the dramatic visitation that I've prayed for, I have had some significant experiences where I felt Joe and knew he was close. One time, a few years after Joe died, I was walking toward my children as they played on the beach with Mamie. As I watched them play, and I enjoyed the sound of the waves and the feel of the cool breeze on my face, I thought of how much Joe loved the beach. My next thought was, *oh how he'd love to be here!* Just as I finished this thought, I had a warm feeling run through me. I said quietly with a smile, "You are here, aren't you?" That warm feeling stayed with me throughout the day and I enjoyed it a little more, knowing he was with us.

My sister, Danette, had another experience with

Joe, this time a little bit more subtle, but nonetheless, a message from him to me. The kids and I flew from Florida to Arizona to be with my family for Christmas. Danette handed me a box to open, after everyone had opened gifts. She also handed me a card which explained the unexpected gift. In the note, she told me that she was buying earrings for someone and there was a half-off special for a second pair. She had a strong impression to buy a pair of ruby studs, but didn't know who she was buying them for. She tried to think of who she knew with a birthday in January that she could give them to but no one came to mind, even though her own daughter, Cynthia, and our sister, Diana, both have January birthdays. Weeks later, when she was packing for her trip to spend Christmas with all of us, she opened the drawer and saw the earrings. It didn't hit her until that moment that they were meant for me and that Joe wanted her to give them to me for our anniversary. I sobbed as I read the letter. I'm so grateful my sister knows how to follow prompting like this.

In 2002 and 2003 Joe made himself known quite a few times. Or was I finally ready to feel him more? Jasmine was baptized in the middle of December and I felt more at peace that week than I've felt in a long time. At one moment, when I was reading to the children, I knew Joe was with us. I felt like he was right in front of me and if I put my hand out, I could possibly touch him.

In the church, we all take accountability for each other. All men are assigned to a few families who they visit once a month and help them with any needs they might have. We were blessed to have Brother Robinson as our "home teacher." He attended Jasmine's baptism and was introduced to Joe that day. Joe's journal entry he wrote after he was baptized has been a part of all the children's baptism programs. I also played one of his tapes where he shares his testimony of Jesus Christ and His church. The next week, when Brother Robinson visited us, he commented on how nice it was to be able to get to know Joe. I was grateful he felt that way. As most home teachers do, he asked if there was any thing he could do for us. I didn't give him anything at the time but called him the next day and asked if he could help me put a certain Christmas gift together. The following is an account of what he experienced in his own words:

Spiritual encounter with Brother Reed:

Dec 2002   12/14/03

About a year ago, Sister Reed asked me, as her home teacher, to become Santa Clause for a day while they were away on a trip so she could surprise J.R.

with a new Basketball Hoop upon their return home from their trip. I was to pick it up from Toys R Us and assemble it then place it in the backyard with a beautiful red bow.

I've put together many a 'Christmas toy' in my day and thought this to be of little challenge for a Santa dad like myself. Boy was I wrong! Much to my surprise, this simple task turned out to be an event that I will never forget. Don't ask me for my opinion on the Huffy companies' ability to translate Chinese. Anyway, when I finally got the box in hand (another long story) I opened it up one cool evening after work figuring I would have no problem assembling it in an hour or two. I began at about 6pm. To make a long story short, at about 10pm, my fuse was running short. The basketball standard was only halfway done and I felt that well known Robinson fuse starting to ignite. Huffy had packaged the box with missing and incorrect parts and directions that looked like they were written and illustrated by the temporary holiday help.

At one point I realized I had put two sections together incorrectly because the lame drawing in the directions was so unclear. I then began to take the pole apart when I jammed my finger on one of the bolts. In a fit of rage, I threw the wrench across the garage and just about let out a very choice expletive. At that instant of my anger release, I felt an overwhelming sense that Joe was standing there across the garage laughing at me. He just pointed at me and belly laughed! I thought to myself, why in a moment of rage would my mind switch over to thinking of Joe? I then realized as I was putting the toy together that I was doing this for Joe because he couldn't be here himself to do this for his son. I then felt an overwhelming calm come over me and a keen sense of the spirit of which I was asked to do this. I realized that I would have done this for my own kids and that Joe needed me to do this for Darla. I know I would have gotten mad putting it together regardless of the situation, but when I felt Joe's presence so strongly, it jolted me back into a sense of feeling honored to do this service. I knew that Joe was laughing because he understands the mortal man that he was and that he would have experienced the same type of emotions any dad experiences when dealing with common "some assembly required" situations.

After calming down I continued for a bit reflecting on the experience I had just had. It was amazing, my change in attitude and the calming effect it had on me. I was no longer concerned about 'getting the job done' so quickly. In fact, I finished it up the next day. It was also amazing how much quicker and smoother the thing went together after that. I'm sure that Joe had a lot to do with that.

I am grateful that there is a way for those that pass on and love us can intervene in our lives for good. I was not only blessed that night to be able to serve my home teaching family but also to experience a thinning of the veil in a way that only a few get to experience. Some may say that my mind created these situations, but I know that it is a true thing that happens to me as I have *encountered this with several of my own deceased relatives.*

I wish the best for the Reed family and I hope they get to experience the closeness to their Husband and Father as I have been so privileged to do.

Alan P. Robinson-

The following August, as I heard talk of fathers giving their children Priesthood blessings before they went back to school, I asked the heavens again, "Why did Joe have to leave us?" I had such a strong desire for Joe to be the one to bless his own children. As I was having a little pity party, I thought about Brother Robinson and knew that the next best thing would be to have him give the children their blessings. He didn't hesitate to accept and make arrangements to come to our home that week. I pleaded with God that day to let Joe come and be a part of the blessings. All the many years of pleading and crying and longing to have a visit from Joe was answered and satisfied that night. It was an experience not to be taken lightly or to be compared with any experience depicted on television shows about mediums and their encounters with those who have died. This was a testimony to me of the power of the priesthood, of God's love for each of us, and of Joe's love and desire to care for his family. Brother Robinson asked me to pray before they gave the blessings. I again prayed for Joe to be able to be with us and as I finished, Brother Robinson softly and humbly declared that Joe was with us and he would be giving us a proxy father's blessing for Joe. There was a peaceful feeling in the room as Brother Robinson and his companion gave the children their blessings. As they finished with Jessica's blessing I felt a need to have my own blessing, as I would also be attending school soon. For many years I had wondered how much Joe is able to be with us. I have complained to Joe many times about how much I have to do by myself and how hard it is. I have questioned his ability to be with us. I know now that Joe was listening and he took this opportunity to respond to my questioning heart. The moment Brother Robinson laid his hands on my head, he hesitated and I could tell he was emotional. He later told me that he felt hands over his and felt someone to his left. As he gained composure and was able to speak, he announced that Joe was with us. He then spoke of Joe's great love for me and told me not to question Joe's love and concern and presence in our home. It was almost a scolding, like Joe was a little peeved with me for even thinking he would not be there for us. He told me that when I was hugging our children he was there hugging them with me and that he would always watch over his children, "for they are a treasure to him" as much as they are to me. Again I had this strong feeling of Joe saying, "Don't question me and my desire to be with you and our children!" He then blessed me with strength and patience. Brother Robinson was really humbled by this experience and grateful to have been an instrument in the Lord's hands in giving me this blessing. This experience is yet another testimony to me of my belief in God, in an after life, and in our loved ones being our own personal angels.

My journal:

4 November 2006

Friday morning I was helping J.R. with his English paper. I talked him into writing it about West Point. We were finishing it up the morning it was due, something I am very familiar with but not what I want my children to get into the habit of doing. He needed to cite where he found his information: the Internet, a West Point book, and his Dad's West Point yearbooks. I picked up one of the yearbooks to look for the editor's name, and happened to grab the 1987 "Howitzer." As I opened the hard front cover, I admired the familiar West Point crest that jumped out at me. The gold crest stood out on the black paper.

Underneath it I noticed something typed in the same gold embossing, it reads: "THE YEAR I MET DARLA." I couldn't believe my eyes! Joe had never shown this to me and I had never noticed it. I never knew it was there. After all these years, this was the first time I had seen it. Tears ran down my smiling face.

I have had a sweet feeling since then. I smile when I think of the message he left for me. I feel like he came back for a visit and said, "Remember how much I love you!" Being reminded of his love sustains me, fills me, and strengthens me. I wouldn't trade a life time with someone else for the brief time I had with Joe.

I have mentioned patriarchal blessings previously. Joe spoke of his blessing many times while he was anticipating fighting in the war. He drew strength from the promises within. I hesitate to write too much about it because it is sacred; it is a written blessing given by a man of God who, through inspiration, tells us what God wants us to know about our life. God reveals to us our talents, our gifts, our callings in life, and our potential. We find out who we really are. It is a powerful message from God, a letter from Him, our own personal scripture from our Father in Heaven.

J.R. got his patriarchal blessing when he was sixteen. Hearing what God has in store for my boy filled my heart with peace, and knowing his potential helped me to look at him with more respect and trust. He was empowered by his blessing, I noticed small changes; he seemed to stand a little taller, physically and spiritually. I would not trade this moment for anything. This was a moment where I thanked God with all my heart for my membership in His church.

I knew Joe was there. He wouldn't have missed it and I knew he would be with us as his daughter received her blessing. So in anticipation of Jasmine's special moment, I wanted to read her daddy's letters and journal with her. I hoped it could help her to know how much he cares for her and will be there for her. I wanted him to be able to inspire her. I walked into her room with an armful of books: the notebook filled with Joe's letters from the war, a huge notebook with his letters to me when we were dating, and a couple of his journals. I announced that we were going to read a page from each book. Jasmine moaned just a bit.

"I don't understand why you don't want to read what your dad has written. Don't you understand the blessing of having all of this?" I asked.

"Mom, I just have a hard time really feeling that I have a dad. I don't know what it feels like and I don't know what it feels like to feel him when he is around. It just doesn't mean anything to me. I don't know him."

Her indifference broke my heart. How could I help her know how much Joe loves her? I couldn't think of anything I hadn't already said so I held out the biggest notebook and said, "Just take this and open it up and pick any letter to read." She reluctantly took it and plopped back down on her bed, rolling her eyes and sighing loudly. She rested the back of the book on her lap with the pages facing upward. Her hands were on both sides of the book and her thumbs ran over the plastic paper protectors before she stuck them in between the pages and parted the book, opening it up in her lap.

She looked down at the words on the page and was silent for a moment, and then surprised me with, "Okay, that's creepy!"

"Excuse me?!"

She read, "'Dearest Darla, Well guess what I am about to do in 20 minutes? Yep, you guessed it, I'm on my way to receive my patriarchal blessing…'"

"Ha!!!" I blurted out. "Your daddy got you good! He heard what you said and he showed you, didn't he?!" I laughed out loud as Jasmine tried to hold her smile back. I could imagine Joe laughing at his daughter and I closed my eyes and saw his beautiful smiling face. "That was perfect!" I smiled at the heavens.

I know this was not a coincidence. I know Joe cares deeply about his children and I hope and pray they will learn this for themselves as they continue to have experiences *with* him and read his precious words.

Dearest Darla,   *15 Jan. '89*
(When I was on my mission)

Well guess what I am about to do in 20 minutes? Yep, you guessed it I'm on my way to receive my patriarchal Blessing from Bro. Field in Newburgh. I decided to share this with you not only because of your obvious interest in what it will say, but also because it has been awhile since I've shared a spiritual experience with you and I think it is important that we share these things with each other. Every letter you write has something of a spiritual nature in it where as mine are more of worldly things. Today in church the theme was on Prayer and how important it is in our lives especially in our relationship with Heavenly Father. Probably my biggest flaw in keeping the commandments is fasting; of course you know my love for eating as much as possible. This week I have been trying to better prepare myself to receive this blessing through prayer, but fasting has always been difficult, well not difficult just not the most pleasant thing for me to do all the time. Anyway I fasted & prayed about this whole event and we'll see what happens in a little while because its time for me to go, so I'll tell you what happens when I return. Bye I love U.

Well, I'm back and Darla this Blessing is more than I ever dreamed it would or could be. I heard things that made so much sense it is scary. My first thoughts were "How does he know so much about me and my past?" I guess it is because it wasn't him that knew, it was Heavenly Father. Darla my Blessing talks about how my parents prepared me in mortality to recognize and accept the Gospel when presented at the appropriate time. I never made mention of any of my past that would prompt him to mention that. There are many other things too, like my field of study (major) in school and how my occupation in life will be in technology. That's right it even includes my occupation and Bro. Field, to this moment, has no idea of what I major in at West Point.

I guess you would like me to get to the parts you are most interested in...☺ Well, I am from the Tribe of Joseph and the House of Manasseh, with the Blessings of the House of Ephraim. Now for the good part...I can't remember word for word but the Blessing talks about how in the Premortal existence I made choices and one of them being the hand of a certain Daughter of God. And from my upbringing and hers she was able to recognize me and I her.... ☺ Now of course that is not word for word but sweetheart that is about what he said... Darla there is so much more that I won't be able to wait for 3 weeks to get it back. So much of it answers many of my questions and thoughts that I have pondered a lot about lately.

I guess receiving this Blessing at a

later age and after attending the Temple has poured so much meaning into it that I can actually look back in my life and see how my past has contributed and will contribute to my future.

When I think of this I think of how my parents especially my mother has been the instrument to prepare me for all this. Heavenly Father must've really trusted Mom. And you know Darla it is ironic that she is the one that is the most opposed to all of this, even after all that she has done. Everything that you liked about me when we first met, I know is because my mother taught me what is good and right...

Well Darla I hope this helps you to gather your thoughts about our situation as you look at your P. Blessing. I know that I am definitely a Happy Camper from this experience; you have no idea how grateful I am for all that has occurred since that cold winter day on the 21st of Feb. 1987. I love you, Sister Cathcart; please remember that!

Je t'aime,

Always,

Joe

The letter he wrote me after he received his blessing in print was conveniently placed right after this one so I read both of them to her.

Feb '89

....I also just received my P-Blessing in the mail, so I'll correctly recite exactly what it says about marriage:

"...While in the pre-existent state, you made many choices and among them was the choice of a fine hand-maiden of the Lord, whom you would recognize quickly when you and she met again in mortality. At your appointed time, you and she will be sealed in a temple of the Lord to be husband and wife, not only in mortality, but for all eternity...."

I guess there really are marriages made in Heaven?

Then it goes on to talk about children etc. Well there you have it, uncut and uncensored. So what do you think? I think it is awfully funny how you and I met 21 years to the date after I entered mortality. ☺ There are other things in my P-Blessing that point to some other peculiarities that have occurred in my life.

I know you're probably trippin' over this stuff, but you might as well take a bottle of chill pills because we still have 2 ½ months left.

Now for the not so great news, if you want to call it news. About all of our traveling & what not, what are your parents gonna think about this ordeal and is it going to matter?? I know mine are trippen' but I am pretty capable of doing as I please despite the pressure. I guess what I'm trying to say is be prepared for the worst, not everyone is going to have that pleasant spirit and understanding that people out in the mission field are blessed with. Some members will be darn right up tight and mean...

Just be prepared for opposition; you know that it is inevitable.

Anyway about the D.C. Temple, we

will go there the day after graduation because I have 3 friends getting married that day and you & I are going to attend! I can't think of a better time to ask about our own broom-jumping decisions, can you?

...Take care Sweetheart! And remember that I Love You!

Always,

Joe

Jessica has since gotten her patriarchal blessing as well. This is, by far, one of the highlights of motherhood! It's such a privilege to hear what God has in store for my children, to hear their potential, to know that they are not only my children but they are literally children of God and He knows them better than I ever will. It has brought me so much peace of mind and joy and it has humbled me to realize what great individuals I have in my home. I'm grateful also for my husband's blessing and the insight it has given to Joe and me and to his children. I love knowing that this life was not where we began and there is so much more to come!

CHAPTER 16

"*Happily Ever After*"
The New Version

From my neighbor, Kim:

February 16, 1998

I have just finished reading letters regarding your dad. My dear little ones J.R., Jasmine and little Jessica...I didn't know your dad. I am a neighbor to you now. I only have seen pictures and seen videos and heard audio tapes of a man who has passed on to a not so distant existence, but now lives on through you, his living legacy.

In J.R. although you are a 5 year old little boy I see your dad in you; the resemblance, the stature, the eyes and the smile. I am sure the way you walk is your dads. I know your dad through you J.R. The desire to be with people, and the tight and endearing love you have for your mother. You love sports especially basketball like your daddy. Today you showed me your daddy's ribbons and medals, you took me into "his room" (It's a closet where your mom has all of your dads stuff.) You talked freely of when he died. You showed me a picture of your dad and I envied you, that you knew him.

Jasmine, you are like your dad in very many ways too. Your beautiful brown skin that reflects the divine diversity that exists in our world. You are a lover of life like your dad...I am sure you have inherited your tenacity from him too! Every time I am near you, you make me laugh. I sat next to you in church yesterday and your mom was struggling to keep you still, you went head first in the pew in front of us to say "hi" to someone...You and Sarah proceeded to wave furiously at Mr. Bob at the sacrament table. I see a very old, wise spirit in you Jasmine that is somewhat frustrated in a 3 year old body! I could only imagine your daddy chasing you around and having really deep discussions with you about life, God and love. I know your dad through you little Jasmine...and I often envy you too, for you knew him.

Sweet dear Jessica... When I look at you Jessica I see your daddy's eyes. They are full of love and an assurance of who you are, why you are here and where you are going. I am sure that before you came to this earth you met your daddy. He probably held you and gave you instructions on life, J.R., Jasmine and to give your mommy lots of kisses! He joined in with the choir of angels that bid you farewell from your heavenly home. You are an embracer. Just like your dad I can tell your passions will be of good works and God. When I first met you, I loved to hold you, and envied you so... for I knew you had seen your dad last. You held your daddy's desire for us to know life will indeed go on...

To you three dear ones, your dad is probably so pleased to know the characteristics you have are so finely *intertwined with those of your mother; whom I know he loves, a love like we read in fairy tales. A love so strong that even death cannot hinder.*

Once on a cold and windy evening as you left my house...I stood to make sure you arrived home 2 houses away...I saw your mom pushing a big stroller with 2 little girls arms and legs busily moving and a young boy walked confidently behind...And in the deep of my mind's eye...I saw your dad...a pace or so behind. The wind felt even chillier and I lingered in the dark...I said in an audible voice, "Hi, Joe..." And I realized I knew him.

Kim Lee Harrington

Many years later, after a long day of editing, I sat at the dinner table with my children. They were excited about all three of them being on the high school track team. They were all practically talking at once, competing to be the one to tell me about their training and whatever happened to them that day. They were messing with each other, laughing and having a great time. I caught only half of the conversation because my mind was still in the past. Because I wanted to be more accurate with the details of our engagement, I had referred to my journal. To read the experiences of those nine or so months was exhausting and I was still reliving some of the emotion and the anxiety I felt at that time when the kids had come busting through the door. I was forced out of that world but my mind couldn't quite fully make the transition. As I sat there, thinking about how overwhelmed I still felt to have just gone through those feelings again, I thought of how much everyone had been worried about our future children. Now, with the perspective of the past in my mind, I had the privilege of fast-forwarding into the future. There they were, right in front of me: happy, healthy, faithful children. I was thinking, "Do you see this Joe? We did it! It all worked out, just look at them! It was all worth it!" I had a strong urge to hug my children and celebrate!

The worries of that day… "They'll be teased and not fit in with either race. Life will be so hard for them…" are so far from reality that it's laughable now. They seem to get more positive attention because of their being bi-racial. Actually they are more than just two races, they are very proud to be African-Cherokee-Indonesian–Portuguese-Scottish-American.

I often share with the kids when I recognize a characteristic of their father's in them. His DNA is so strong that I'm pointing things out on a regular basis!

JR looks more like Joe every day. He makes the

same faces, he walks like him, laughs like him and he likes and dislikes the same foods. He's also passionate about working out, just like his dad. He has been pushing himself for years, and it paid off his junior year in track. He took third place at state in the 110 and 300 hurdle events, and helped his team take the state title. His senior year he would have taken state if he hadn't had a couple injuries. He also reminds me of Joe as he is able to, in a light hearted manner, respond to negative comments thrown his way and leave everyone with a smile if not a laugh. When his sisters want to "go-off" on him, he usually has a funny comment to change their mood. He makes it impossible to be angry with him for too long. One time when I was lecturing him on how to clean his bathroom better, I told him I would return with a white glove test. He piped in, "Mom, you know you don't need the glove." (I'm white enough.) His charm continues to make me smile. He has also followed in his father's footsteps by being faithful. When he was three, his daddy and I asked him what song he wanted to sing before we had our family night lesson. He said "Hi Ho," so, Joe and I started singing the seven dwarfs" song, "Hi ho, hi ho, it's off to work we go…" JR stopped us and tried to correct us a couple times before we realized that he wanted us to sing, "I hope they call me on a mission, when I have grown a foot or two…" He still likes that song and the idea of serving the Lord. He has now grown "a foot or two" and is looking forward to serving a two-year mission in Ghana. He hopes to do hurdles for a college when he returns from his mission, and has the goal of getting his master's degree. I know J.R. will be successful because he has already expressed his desire to be a good husband and father and provide for his future family. Besides loving him I really do like my son, I like the person he has become.

Some people say Jasmine looks like me, others say she looks exactly like her father. The only thing I'm sure of is that she most definitely has more than physical characteristics of her father. They both have drive, determination, discipline, athleticism, quick wit and an amazing memory. Jasmine also has the confidence her father had. She makes friends with about everyone around her and she stands firm with her standards, no matter the pressure. She also wants to see others happy, whether it involves hard work or thinking of something funny to say, she'll do what it takes to cheer up a friend. Jasmine is a born leader. She had the goal of being the president of the United States from second to eighth grade. She was an awesome student council president for her K-8 school and has continued to be in leadership positions— in school, in church, and on the volleyball court. As serious as this all sounds, Jasmine is still my comic relief and plays that role with everyone around her. Her chicken costume is a great example of this, she not only wore it for Halloween, but for every fund raiser at "Chick fil-A" and crazy dress-up day at school. You can't help but laugh when someone is in a head-to-toe chicken costume. I know Jasmine will be amazing at whatever she decides to be and do and she'll have a blast doing it. I like her too and I hope to have a morsel of her confidence, discipline, and tenacity someday.

Every time I see Jessica asleep I see my husband's features: the shape of his face, his jaw line, his chin and especially his pouty mouth. Joe sang well. He did some duets for church and sang in the church choir, but Jessica has taken it to another level! She has been blessed with a beautiful voice and an ability to learn songs incredibly fast. She is a performer and I am amazed with her talent! She loves to be on stage, the bigger the crowd, the better! She won the title of Miss Arizona Pre-Teen when she was 13, and she had to do it all on her own because she does not have a pageant mom! She even dealt with opposition from us! We were usually annoyed with her practicing and constant pageant research online. Jasmine gave her the most grief but she sure coached her the week before and cheered louder than anyone when her sister was on that stage! She also has the desire to stand up for what is right and to follow the Lord. I'm grateful to Jessica who continues to remind me to slow down and look for the flowers. And yes, I like her as much as I love her and I feel it a blessing and privilege to be her mother.

Most happily-ever-after stories end with someone getting married and "riding off into the sunset." This one is different. I haven't really put too much effort towards finding anyone. Remember? I gave that job to God, but I guess He didn't want it, or maybe the order I placed was too tall. I've continued to go back and forth with whether I'd be capable of loving another man. My main concern has been our children's well being. They are a huge part of the happily-ever-after story. Despite the physical absence of their father, they have his attributes and his character and his desire to follow God. His legacy most definitely lives on through them.

And this is the rest of the happily-ever-after story...

I recently found another letter from Joe which he had written to me during our engagement:

10 July 1988

...I wish so bad that we were holding hands across the altar right now! Can't you see it Darla ☺ Us looking into the mirrors and seeing just you and me forever and ever and ever...Sometimes all I dream about is that painting we're gonna have made with me leading you, and children following us with all of us

holding hands on our way up to see Heavenly Father. Oh Darla can't you just picture it? When we finally retire and the children are all grown up and we have "our house" I'm gonna have it painted and put it in the living room so it is the first thing everyone see's as they enter in.

I Love you so much Darla, I get exhausted trying to think of different ways to say it. I just want to show you now. The talking is getting a little old and it is soon time for action. I just want to marry you! That's all!

Loving you Eternally,

Joe

The painting Joe wanted to have in our home is a depiction of a dream a prophet describes in the Book of Mormon. In his dream he saw a path with an iron rod leading to a beautiful tree, which he followed. Once he arrived at the tree, he tasted the fruit on the tree and then turned to call for his family because he wanted them to taste the delicious fruit as well. Every aspect of his dream symbolizes our journey through life. Keeping God's commandments keeps us on the path. The iron rod symbolizes the guidance and stability the scriptures provide. The tree of life and the fruit is symbolic of the love of God. In the dream he beckons his family to come taste of the fruit of the tree of life. He wants his family to feel the love of God as he has felt it. He directs them to stay on the path, holding onto the iron rod for safety and direction through the "mists of darkness" (temptations). I will cherish the words my husband has left behind because there is this message in almost every letter, every journal entry, and every tape he made. As the father of our family, he continues to lead by example. He knew of the love of God and how happy it made him and he continues to beckon us to taste of it also through the words he has left behind.

When Joe died, there were so many dreams that were taken from us. He was supposed to take me to Italy, he wanted to coach his children's basketball team, he had a goal to be able to dunk with his son, and we dreamed of serving a mission together. Those first few devastating years, I was painfully aware of all the dreams that were taken away. But Joe has continued to remind me of what was not taken. The eternal dreams we made did not die with him. Our eternal goals have not changed. We were married for time and all eternity. Though Joe and I are physically separated, I know he will continue to help me and I know that our reunion will be sweet and we will continue on with our relationship and our progression together. Our love and our union will never end.

My Dear Sweet Wife,   *23 Feb 1991*

I Love You! Today I'll probably get mail from you for the last time for a long while. So I'm answering it now. Sweetheart, tomorrow I go to combat, which you've probably known now for a month. The thing that I would most like you to know about me is that my first and foremost goal in this life is to make it so you and I get back to the presence of our Heavenly Father and reside in his highest mansions. I know now that that is the only significant thing I can ever do in this life. Everything else just does not matter any more.

I am eternally grateful for having met you and sacrificed the things I have that I might have you as my Bride. Once again, I can't wait to have children with you and to learn and grow from the challenges they will present to us as we struggle to teach them the Gospel that they might come to know the goodness of our Father in

Heaven and his Son Jesus Christ as we know it.

Sweetheart I am very scared right now. As we prepare our things most everyone is keeping to themselves and preparing mentally for the mission. All I can do is pray and hope and not doubt!!

I will probably write you many times more however the mail is so messed up that the letters will take forever to get to you. Remember that I Love You and that no matter what happens, "We will be together forever someday".

Loving You for All Eternity
Your Eternal Companion,

Joe

Our story continues…

Happily Ever After!

ABOUT THE AUTHOR

©SVB Photography, LLC =SVBphoto.com=

Darla Reed is currently living in Peoria, Arizona with her two daughters, Jasmine and Jessica. Her son, JR, is serving a 2-year mission in Ghana, Africa for The Church of Jesus Christ of Latter Day Saints. Darla received her BA in Integrative Studies, Health and Business in 2007 from Arizona State University. She is now a Manager with Lifewave, and enjoys working in the natural health industry.

HisWordsByDarlaReed.blogspot.com
Facebook.com/pages/his-words

Made in the USA
Las Vegas, NV
21 January 2021

16302879R00219